THE RIGHT WAY TO
PLAY CHESS

THE RIGHT WAY
TO
PLAY CHESS

D B Pritchard

RIGHT WAY

CONTENTS

INTRODUCTION

The Right Way To Play Chess has now served as tutor to a whole generation of readers and it is a continual source of satisfaction to me to be approached by young, and sometimes not-so-young experts and be told that their introduction to the game was through this book.

Chess is perennial but not changeless. Many developments have taken place in the game during the last forty years and these have been reflected in succeeding editions of *The Right Way To Play Chess*. It may therefore comfort you to know that this book was right up to date at the time of going to press and for practical purposes is likely to remain so for a few years at least, by which time, if past experience is to be relied on, it will be overtaken by a new edition.

Chess is not an easy game, but any idea that you have to be highly intelligent or "clever" to play it should be dismissed. If the game were easy to master, it would be trivial and would attract little interest. On the other hand, if chess were hard to learn it would not be played – and often played well – by six- and seven-year-olds. The magic of chess is that it can be learnt by almost anyone, played almost anywhere and at almost any level with equal enjoyment.

The developments in the game over the past forty years,

to which I referred above, have been exciting ones. Chess has suddenly become both respectable and popular.

The World Championship match at Reykjavik in 1972 between Bobby Fischer and Boris Spassky attracted world-wide publicity, though admittedly for reasons not wholly to do with chess. This accelerated the boom which had started years before and which, against many predictions, has yet to show signs of a decline. Chess, it appears, is here to stay; not just as an indoor game but as a major field of intellectual activity with wide support from educationalists as well as the public at large.

Millions of people – literally – play at home in the family circle and with friends but never take the game seriously. At the other end of the spectrum there is a growing body of chess professionals, in Europe and the Americas in particular. In between these two groups are what may be called the club players who vary from the man who turns out occasionally for his works' team to the enthusiast who gives most of his spare time to the game and enters for every event in the calendar.

The standard of play, certainly at the higher levels and probably at the club level as well, has risen remarkably. Whereas thirty or so years ago the international scene was dominated by a handful of masters, now there is a small army of them and behind them another, larger army of players only marginally below master strength.

How has this come about? The explanation is easy to find: youth has taken the game for its own. If you look in today on almost any chess event you will be struck by the number of young players, many of school age, taking part. This phenomenon is the natural outcome of the rapid growth of chess clubs and chess teaching in schools that has taken place since the war. The image of chess as an old man's game has quietly died.

In the World Olympiads – the Olympic Games of chess

– teams representing over a hundred nations regularly compete; and here too youth is very much in evidence.

At no period in its long history has the game been so intensely studied as at present. Recent researches have led to many theoretical advances, particularly in the opening phase (chess openings, since they begin from a standard position, lend themselves more readily to analysis than other stages of the game). Old ideas have been challenged, techniques perfected, styles modified, fashions changed.

Yet it is true to say that the basics of the game remain invariable and *The Right Way To Play Chess* is as relevant today as when it was first written. The book is planned to take the complete beginner to the standard expected of a good club player. The journey should be a pleasant one, for chess is above all a game and a game is to be enjoyed. A chess set is necessary to follow the text. A plain wooden or plastic set is best. The type known as Staunton pattern is the most widely used and is recommended.

The final chapter gives some general information for the reader who wishes to take the game seriously. It is necessarily brief, but hopefully provides sufficient insight into the exciting world of competitive chess to encourage further enquiry.

It would be wrong to leave this introduction without a brief mention of the history of the game. The precise origins of chess are obscure and are still being debated. Almost certainly, however, a four-handed game of ancient India known as chaturanga is a distant ancestor. From chaturanga was developed a two-player version, called shatranj, the true forerunner of our chess. The game reached Europe via Persia and the Arab lands by about the 9th century, and for many hundreds of years remained a pastime of the rich and privileged. Popular interest in the game spread as cheap printing made communication easier and technical advances afforded greater leisure.

Over the centuries the rules of the game have benefited from many changes, and even today minor amendments are made from time to time as chess remains for millions indisputably the best two-player game in the world. This is something that will not change.

In this new, and completely revised edition of *The Right Way To Play Chess*, the modern and now internationally-approved method of recording game moves has been adopted.

D.B.P.

1

HOW THE GAME
IS PLAYED

The Game

The game of chess is played between two players or parties on a board of sixty-four squares (8 x 8) alternately coloured light and dark (normally black and white).

Each player has at his command a force of sixteen men; *eight pieces* (one king, one queen, two rooks, two bishops, two knights) and *eight pawns*. The opposing forces are usually coloured, and are referred to as White and Black.

Players move in turn, and the object of the game is to capture (checkmate) the opposing king.

Each chessman is governed by its own rules of movement and is now examined separately.

The King (♔♚)

The king moves one square in any direction (diagram 1), but since he takes seven moves to cross the board he is a comparatively weak piece. However, the importance of the king is evident from the previous paragraph – his loss entails the loss of the game.

The king may not therefore be moved onto a square attacked by an opposing man. If the king is attacked (i.e., if he is *threatened with capture* on the next move), he is said to be "in check", and the opponent may, but is not obliged to say "check" when making the move that attacks the king.

The player whose king is threatened *must immediately move out of check*. There are three methods of doing this:

(1) By moving the king onto a square not attacked by an enemy man.

(2) By capturing the attacking unit, either with the king or with another man.

(3) By moving a man between the king and the attacker.

DIAGRAM 1

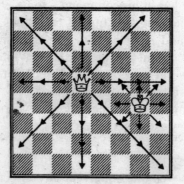

THE KING AND QUEEN

Not all these resources may be available. If none are playable – that is, if the king has no square to which to move out of check, the attacking man may not be captured and no man may be interposed – then the king is said to be "checkmated", or, simply "mated", and the game is over. Note that the king is the only piece that can never *actually* be captured – the game is concluded when capture is inevitable.

A king may capture an opposing man by moving onto the square on which it stands, simultaneously removing it from the board. Since it is illegal for the king to move into check, only an undefended man may be so captured. Capturing in chess is not compulsory (as in draughts), and there is no "huffing" or jumping over the captured man. The two kings must not stand on adjacent squares, since both would then be in check from each other.

The Queen (♕♛)

The queen moves in any direction across any number of squares that may be vacant (diagram 1). Her move is an extension of the king's move, limited only by the confines of the board. She is the most powerful of the pieces.

The queen captures in the same manner as the king, but since she is not liable to check, she may capture a man that is defended, although such a movement is unusual, as, being the most powerful piece, the queen is rarely surrendered voluntarily for a piece other than the opposing queen. It will be seen that the queen, if centrally placed, controls almost half of an unrestricted board.

The Rook (♖♜)

The rook, sometimes referred to as the castle, may move in a *vertical* or *horizontal* direction only, over any number of squares that may be vacant (diagram 2). It captures in the same manner as the queen, occupying the square on which the hostile man stands, whilst removing it from the board. Note that wherever a rook stands on an empty board, it commands fourteen squares.

The Bishop (♗ ♝)

The bishop moves *diagonally* only, over any number of squares that may be vacant, capturing in the same manner as the preceding pieces (diagram 2). Note that a bishop is restricted to the squares of one colour only, and that the nearer it stands to the edge of the board, the fewer the squares it controls.

DIAGRAM 2

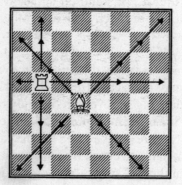

THE ROOK AND BISHOP

From the foregoing it will be clear that the queen combines the moves of rook and bishop. If the queen is moved vertically or horizontally over an odd number of squares, she will then command diagonals of the opposite colour, a property with which the bishop is not endowed.

The Knight (♘♞)

The move of the knight occasions some beginners difficulty. The move is best defined as from one corner of a 3 x 2 rectangle to the opposite corner. Diagram 3 should make this clear.

Men standing on intervening squares do not affect the knight's move. For this reason, some players talk of a knight "jumping" other men.

DIAGRAM 3

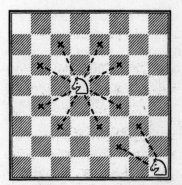

THE KNIGHT

The knight captures in occupying, as is the case with the other pieces. It is strongest on a crowded board, when it can pursue its designs unimpeded, and is very much weaker on an open board when the mobility of the other pieces is proportionately increased.

It will be noted, also, that the knight, like the king, queen and bishop, controls fewer squares when stationed on or near the edge of the board. Also, that if on a white square it controls only black squares and vice versa.

Until the knight becomes familiar, it is not easy to anticipate its movements and in consequence there is a tendency amongst beginners to over-estimate its powers.

The Pawn (♙ ♟)

The pawn, unlike the pieces, moves in a forward direction only, one square at a time.

Each pawn has, however, the option of moving two squares forward on its first move, and this right is retained throughout the game, always provided the pawn has not been moved.

The pawn, alone of all the chessmen, captures in a different manner to which it moves. Whereas it *moves* one square straight forward, it *captures* one square diagonally forward. A pawn may not move diagonally forward unless, in so doing, it captures an opposing man; nor may it move straight forward, either one or two squares, unless such squares are vacant.

The initial double move of the pawn was introduced to stimulate what would otherwise be a slow game. However, in order that a pawn should not take advantage of the double move to evade a hostile pawn, a rule, known as the *en passant* (Fr.: "in passing") rule was introduced.

This lays down that if a pawn, moving two squares forward from its initial position, could have been captured by an opposing pawn *if it had only moved one square,* then such capture may be effected as if the pawn had only moved one square. The pawn making the initial double move is removed from the board and the capturing pawn occupies the square that the captured pawn would have occupied had it only moved one. The right to make a capture *en passant* is forfeited if not exercised immediately Note that a pawn can only be captured *en passant* by another pawn, and not by a piece.

A pawn on reaching the end of the board (the last rank of eight squares) is promoted to any piece (other than a king) that the player chooses. A queen is the natural selection, in view of her being the strongest piece, but occasionally the peculiarity of the position demands promotion to knight, or even to bishop or rook.

No restriction is placed on the number of pawn-promotions, and although eight such promotions are possible, it is very rare that more than one or two occur in a game.

Examine the diagram (4). In this, as in all other diagrams in this book (and commonly in all chess literature) White is assumed to be playing UP the board, Black DOWN the board. For purposes of economy, four separate positions are given on the one diagram, but in each case the whole of the board is assumed to be included.

DIAGRAM 4

BLACK

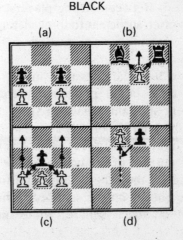

WHITE

THE PAWN

In (a) none of the four pawns can move. In (b) the white pawn can capture either the rook or the bishop, or it can move straight ahead onto the white square. In each of these cases it has reached the eighth rank, or end of the board, and must be simultaneously promoted to a piece which is placed on the square to which the pawn moves. If a queen is desired, and the white queen is still on the board, a reversed rook or a coin will serve the purpose.

In (c) the white pawns stand in their initial positions, as will be clear from diagram 5. Hence the two outside pawns can both be advanced one or two squares. Both can also capture the black pawn. The black pawn can capture either of these two pawns, whilst the middle white pawn is unable to move.

In (d) the white pawn has just made the initial double move, and Black can consequently capture *en passant* as shown.

In contrast to knights, pawns tend to be underestimated by beginners. Do not shed pawns lightly: every one is a potential queen. Between strong players, an extra pawn on one side is often sufficient to force victory.

Initial Position

Having seen how the chessmen move, let us now set them up in their initial positions, preparatory to the commencement of a game (diagram 5).

Note that the board is oriented so that there is a black square in the left-hand corner of each player.

In the four corners of the board are the rooks, next to them the knights, then the bishops and finally the royal couples – the queens on the squares of their own colour (black queen on black square, white queen on white square).

Notice carefully the asymmetrical arrangement of the kings and queens – each piece opposite its rival counterpart. The pawns are arrayed in front of their respective pieces.

DIAGRAM 5

BLACK

WHITE

THE INITIAL POSITION

In chess, White always moves first (choice of colour is decided by sortilege: it is common for one player to conceal two pawns, one white and one black in clenched fists, the opponent then choosing "which hand" to determine forces).

Before we can start playing an actual game, however, there are one or two more important rules to be learned; after which it will be necessary to become familiar with a few rudimentary manoeuvres. Chess, to be learnt properly, must be studied step by step, each point being thoroughly assimilated before passing on to the next one, too rapid advancement leading only to confusion and eventual frustration.

Castling

Castling is a privilege to which both sides are entitled once in a game. The manoeuvre, which is a joint move of king and one rook, counts as a single move. It may be played only if all the following conditions are fulfilled:

(1) Neither the king nor the rook have moved.
(2) The king is not in check.
(3) There are no pieces, either hostile or friendly, between the king and the rook, nor does an enemy man attack a square over which, or onto which the king must move.

There is a misconception that one may not castle once the king has been in check. This is incorrect: provided that, in getting out of check the king was not moved (thereby contravening (1) above), castling is permitted.

In castling, the king is first moved two squares in the direction of the rook, which is brought over next to the king on the inside. The move is then complete.

Castling may take place on either side of the board, and is referred to as K-side castling and Q-side castling. Once castling is complete the pieces reassume their normal functions and the manoeuvre cannot be retracted.

The object of the move is two-fold: to bring a rook into play in the centre of the board and to give greater security to the king. The manoeuvre is commonly used by both players during a game.

Examine diagram 6. White may castle on *either* side (the movements of the pieces are indicated by arrows), whereas Black may not castle at all, since the rook on the Q-side has been moved, and to castle K-side the black king would have to pass over a square commanded by an enemy piece (the white bishop).

DIAGRAM 6

BLACK

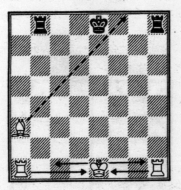

WHITE

CASTLING

Checkmate

We have seen that if a king is attacked (in check) and cannot be moved out of check, and the attacking unit cannot be removed or a friendly man interposed, the king is assumed to be captured (checkmated, or mated) and the game is over.

Here are four examples in each of which the black king is mated. In diagram 7 (a) the black king is attacked by the white queen, which also controls all the neighbouring squares. Since the white queen is protected by the white king she may not be captured, and Black has consequently lost the game. In (b) the black king is attacked by the advanced white pawn, which is defended by the second white pawn. The knight controls the two remaining squares in the vicinity of the king ("the king's field"), who is therefore checkmated.

DIAGRAM 7

BLACK

WHITE

CHECKMATE

In (c) the black king is again attacked, this time by the white bishop, which also indirectly guards the rook, as if the black king captured the rook he would still be in check, and, as we have seen, this would constitute an illegal move. The white rook controls no less than four of the squares in the king's field, the only two remaining escape squares being occupied by black men. The pawn is unable to move (remember, White is playing UP the board, Black is playing DOWN), and the black bishop, only capable of moving on white squares, is unable to intervene. Both the black men are restricting the movements of the black king, and are said to be creating "self-blocks".

In (d) the position is more complex and should be examined carefully. The black king is attacked by the white rook, which is also indirectly defending the knight. The white king controls two escape squares, the bishop one and the knight one. Neither the black rook nor the black knight can capture the attacking piece, nor can either interpose between it and the black king. Black is checkmated. Note that if the black rook and knight were interchanged, either of them would be able to move onto the black square between the black king and the hostile rook. If, in the position given, the black knight was not on the board, the black king would still be checkmated, since the white knight attacks the vacated square.

If the black rook was off the board, however, the black king would be able to move out of check into the corner. All the white pieces are indispensable to the mate.

Stalemate

Occasionally a position arises (usually when there are only a few pieces left on the board) when one side, whose turn it is to move, is unable to do so. If the king were in check, the position would be checkmate. If, however, the king is not in check, the position is known as stalemate, and the game is adjudged a draw.

In diagram 8 (a) the white queen controls the three squares in the king's field, *but she is not attacking the king*. If Black has no other pieces on the board, the position would be stalemate with Black to move. In (b), similarly, the bishops control the king's escape squares. Neither the pawn nor the king can move, and if it is Black's turn to play, White is said to have stalemated Black and the game is a draw.

DIAGRAM 8

BLACK

(a)   (b)

(c)   (d)

WHITE

STALEMATE

In (c), the black king's only square is next to the white king – to occupy which would be an illegal move. A move by the black bishop would expose the king to an attack from the white rook – again illegal. The black rook is in the same dilemma; any move exposing the king to check from the white bishop. These two black pieces are said to be "pinned". As neither can move, with Black's turn to play the game is drawn. If it were White's turn to play, however, the bishop could capture the rook delivering checkmate.

In (d) it will be seen that none of the black men can

move – the pawns obstructing the pieces. Black, to play, is stalemated. The possibility of such a position as this occurring in an actual game is remote.

Stalemates are not common in chess, although the threat of stalemate (or rather, self-stalemate) by the player with the weaker force is often encountered.

Other Methods of Concluding a Game

Apart from checkmate and stalemate, there are several other ways by which a game may be concluded.

(1) INSUFFICIENT FORCE

If neither side has sufficient force left to checkmate the opposing king, the game is drawn. What constitutes insufficient force will be explained in the next chapter.

(2) PERPETUAL CHECK

If one side is able to submit the enemy king to a perpetual series of checks, the game is drawn. Clearly it will not be to the advantage of the stronger side to resort to a "perpetual" (as perpetual check is more commonly called).

(3) REPETITION OF MOVES

If the same position occurs three times in a game, with the same player to move in each case, either side may claim a draw.

(4) FIFTY MOVE RULE

If each side has played 50 consecutive moves without making a capture or pawn move, either player may, on turn, claim a draw. This rule is designed to limit aimless play. The number of moves has recently been extended to 75 in certain specified cases.

(5) DRAW BY MUTUAL AGREEMENT

A draw may be agreed between the players at any stage of the game. Positions are often reached where neither player can lay claim to a winning advantage, and both players are reluctant to embark on doubtful ventures. In such positions, a draw is commonly agreed. A high percentage of master games finish in this way.

(6) RESIGNATION

A player who sees the position is hopeless, and that checkmate is inevitable sooner or later, will "resign" (concede) the game. More than half of all chess games conclude in this manner.

In point of fact, it is advisable for the beginner not to resign, as more can be learnt from being checkmated a few dozen times. Later, however, resignation in irredeemable positions is desirable. A few novices consider that holding out to the bitter end constitutes courage. On the contrary, chess etiquette requires that a player who is clearly beaten shall resign in good grace. A player who continues the struggle can only be prolonging the game in the hope that his opponent will make a mistake – a discourteous imputation of an adversary's ability. But, to repeat, every game should be played to a finish in the initial stages of instruction.

In addition to those given above, there are some other ways in which the result of a game may be determined. These, however, have only to do with such matters as the players' conduct and necessary legal niceties associated with match and tournament games, and they need not concern us here.

Chess Notation

It is one of the merits of chess that moves can be

recorded. We are thereby not only the fortunate inheritors of the great games of past generations but we also have access to the day-by-day battles of modern masters. In the comfort of your own home you can recreate world championship encounters and, if you wish, keep a record of your own games for future amusement or study.

Systems of recording moves are known as notations. There are two common notations; the Algebraic, now in general use and alone sanctioned by the world chess authority, and the Descriptive (or English) notation, still favoured by many players and commonly met with in older chess books. The Descriptive notation, together with the Forsyth notation (used for recording positions), are explained in Chapter 9.

The Algebraic Notation

It is convenient, for reference purposes, to divide the chessboard into eight files (vertical lines of eight squares) and eight ranks (horizontal lines of eight squares). In the algebraic notation the files are lettered a to h from left to right and the ranks are numbered from 1 to 8 bottom to top, using as datum the near left-hand corner of the board when seen from White's side (see diagram 9). Thus every square of the chessboard can be described by a unique letter-and-figure (in that order) combination. For example, in the starting position (diagram 5) White's queen stands on d1 and Black's king on e8. The board is also notionally divided vertically into two halves, the king's side and the queen's side. Viewed from White's side, the king's side is the right half of the board and the queen's side the left half. We have already met this distinction in our discussion of castling.

The men are identified in algebraic notation by their initial letters: K (king); Q (queen); R (rook); B (bishop); N (knight: to distinguish it from the king) and P (pawn).

Chess Moves

We now have a system for identifying men and squares. All that is needed in addition in order to record games is a few symbols to indicate different types of moves. Just to confuse things a little, there are two types of algebraic notation, the long and the short. The only difference between them is that in the long algebraic a move is described in full, whereas in the short algebraic the move is abbreviated. The long algebraic is now little used as it is cumbersome and takes up more space. However, since it is clearer it will be used until Chapter 3 when a switch will be made to the shortened form.

In the long algebraic, the initial of the man moved is given first followed by the square on which it stands. Then a dash (—) to indicate a move to a vacant square, followed by the description of the square moved to. If a man is captured in the process, the dash is replaced by a cross (x) to indicate this. Notice that no ambiguity can arise because no more than one man can ever occupy a square.

Other symbols, common to both long and short notations, are:

+ or ch	=	check
‡ or mate	=	checkmate
0–0	=	castles (king's side)
0–0–0	=	castles (queen's side)

and by way of annotation:

! (exclamation)	=	good move;
? (interrogation)	=	bad move.

A few situations are abbreviated; e.g., e.p. = *en passant*.

DIAGRAM 9

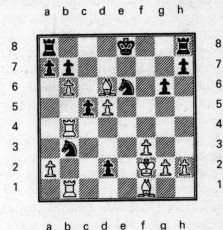

THE ALGEBRAIC NOTATION

Now for a few examples. Look at diagram 9. If in this
position White advanced the pawn at a2 two squares the
move would be transcribed Pa2–a4, while if instead this
pawn captured the knight, the move would be recorded as
Pa2xb3. If White checks with the bishop (only one bishop
can check) the move would be Bf1–b5 ch. If Black chose
to move the queen's rook next to the king, the description
would be Ra8–d8 while if the advanced black pawn is
promoted to queen this move would be recorded as Pd2–
d1(Q). At first, this may seem a bit complicated but
fluency will come with a little practice.

Conclusion

If you have read this chapter at a single sitting, you will probably be in a state of near mental exhaustion. You have possibly already forgotten how the knight moves, or what stalemate is; but you should not let this worry you.

You have the consolation of knowing that there are only a few very minor rules still to be learned, the rest of the book being devoted to the right way to play the game.

The chapter should be re-read carefully after a short interval, and before going on, you should be thoroughly conversant with the moves of the pieces, pawn promotion, check and checkmate, stalemate, castling and chess notation. A good idea is to place half-a-dozen pieces haphazardly on the board and move them around, black and white alternately, capturing, checking, and, if possible, securing positions in which checkmate or stalemate may be given. Then try recording moves as you go along.

By way of a test, return to diagram 9 and see how many of the following questions you can answer correctly: (answers at foot of page):

(1) How many men in the position given are unable to move?

(2) To how many squares can the white bishop on d6 move?

(3) How many men are on their original squares?

(4) Can White play Kf2–e1?

(5) If Black captures the pawn on b6 with the pawn at a7, how should this move be recorded?

(6) On the whole board how many possible (i.e., legal) black moves are there (count the pawn promotion as one move)?

Solutions to Test (Chapter 1)

(1) One. The black pawn at b7.

(2) Eight, including the pawn capture.

(3) Ten: White Bf1, Pa2, Pg2, Ph2.
Black Ke8, Ra8, Rh8, Pa7, Pb7, Ph7.

(4) No: because the white king would then be in check from the black pawn.

(5) Pa7xb6.

(6) Twenty-nine.

2

RUDIMENTARY THEORY

Relative Values of the Chessmen

The reader will no doubt have gathered by this time that the chessmen, being possessed of intrinsic qualities of movement and capture, may also be compared, one with the other, on the yardstick of relative values.

The correlation of the powers of the pieces is deceptive, however, as in any position each man will be possessed of a power peculiar to that position. In diagram 9, page 29, for example, both black rooks are out of play, whereas the humble pawn on d2, threatening, if unwatched, to become a queen, is an apparent force. However, the pawn may soon fall, and the black rooks may bring their long-range guns to bear down the vital files. A game is therefore in a permanent state of flux, and force values change from move to move. The scale of relative values can only remain a guide for the exchange of pieces (an exchange is when one side captures an opposing man, giving up one of its own men in the process) when other considerations are approximately equal. The ability to assess the true value of a position and, in consequence, the extempore values of the men composing the position, is a gift with which only really strong chess-players are endowed.

The king, since he cannot be captured, and is only used as an attacking piece towards the end of the game when his powers are approximately equal to those of a bishop, is excluded from the assessment.

Queen	=	two Rooks
Bishop	=	Knight
Rook	=	Bishop (or Knight) and two Pawns
Bishop (or Knight)	=	three Pawns

These are approximations. The bishop is normally worth a fraction more than the knight and two rooks fractionally more than a queen.

Basic Positions
(a) The Pin

As we have seen in position (c), diagram 8, a piece is pinned if, in moving, it would expose the king to a hostile check. In diagram 10 (a), the knight is also said to be pinned, for although it may be legally moved, the white bishop would then capture the black queen which would be a poor bargain for Black even should the bishop then succumb.

The term "pin" is thus extended to signify any position in which the movement of a man would expose another man to attack from a weaker piece. If there was another black knight at c7 (that is, on the diagonal between the queen and the other knight), the set-up would be known as a half-pin as the movement of either knight would automatically result in the pinning of the other.

(b) Double Check

In the second example (diagram 10 (b)) we see a

double check, when a king is exposed to attack from two hostile men simultaneously. White has just moved the rook, as indicated. In a double check the king must move, since he cannot capture both attacking men or interpose two of his own men in one move. If he cannot move, as in the diagram, he is checkmated. Note that Black can apparently capture either piece with the rook, or interpose a piece between either the king and rook or the king and bishop, but none of these resources are open to him because whichever he adopts the king will still be in check from the remaining white piece.

DIAGRAM 10

BLACK

(a)   (b)

(c)   (d)

WHITE

RUDIMENTARY MANOEUVRES

The extraordinary power of the double check is apparent, and it is something a player should endeavour to avoid unless he is certain that such check would be innocuous – which is very rarely the case.

(c) Discovered Check

This is similar to the double check, but not as dangerous, as the piece moved does not itself give check. If in diagram 10 (b), the white rook had moved to f7 instead of f8 it would then have been a "discovered" and not a "double" check. Black could thus have avoided mate, but would have lost the queen.

(d) The Skewer

The position in 10 (c) is something to guard against. Here the black king, in check, is compelled to move, when the bishop will capture the black queen.

(e) The Fork

The knight, by virtue of its irregular move, can create an embarrassing attack known as a "fork". In the position 10 (d), the knight is attacking both king and queen, and as the king must move out of check, the queen is doomed. The most common fork of the knight is of king and rook, when the rook, which, as we have seen, is the stronger piece, is lost. Forks by other pieces are possible. In diagram 4 (b) for example, the white pawn has forked the black rook and bishop. The term is self-explanatory.

Endings

In order to acquaint the reader with the practical power of the pieces, we will examine one or two game endings.

Assuming that Black has only a king left, White will be able to force mate with a minimum force of:

(1) King and queen. The white king will, of course, be on the board. If White has a pawn which he can safely promote, then it can be reckoned as a queen.

(2) King and rook.

(3) King and two bishops.

(4) King, bishop and knight.

Mate cannot be forced against a lone king with:

(1) King alone – this is obvious.
(2) King and bishop.
(3) King and knight or king and two knights.
(4) Certain positions involving pawns.

It is interesting to observe that two knights (the joy of the novice!) are unable to force mate, whereas a mere pawn which can be promoted is sufficient for the purpose.

King and Queen v. King

Let us examine the system of forcing mate by king and queen against a bare king.

This performance should not demand more than ten moves, in most positions considerably fewer (when one talks of moves in chess one means moves of both sides).

Place the white king on e1, the white queen on e8, and the black king on g5. White can mate in a number of ways, but the principle remains the same in every case – the lone king must be driven to the edge of the board where the queen will deliver the mate, the white king assisting.

A series of checks with the queen will achieve nothing (all beginners assume that checks are stronger than quiet moves (i.e., moves that are not checks), in the hope, presumably, that "it might be mate"). White therefore moves Qe8–f7!, restricting the movements of the doomed monarch.

Notice that in chess, moves are numbered in pairs.

White	Black
1. Qe8–f7	Kg5–g4

Not Kg5–h4, when Qf7–g6, further restricting the king.

2. Ke1–f2	**Kg4–g5**
3. Kf2–g3	**Kg5–h6**

The only square.

4. Qf7–g8

4. Kg3–f4? would be a grave error since the black king would then be without a move – stalemated, in other words – and the game would be drawn.

4. ...	**Kh6–h5**

Again the only move.

5. Kg3–f4	**Kh5–h6**

Not Kh5–h4 allowing White to mate immediately.

6. Kf4–f5

And now mate next move is unavoidable.

6. ...	**Kh6–h5**
7. Qg8–g5 mate	

The black king has been forced to the edge of the board and is there checkmated. King and queen cannot mate a bare king anywhere except at the side: the same applies to king and rook against bare king, as the following example shows.

King and Rook v. King

Set up the kings as before, and substitute a white rook for the queen. Since this mate is more difficult, as might be expected, and as it is one which you are likely to encounter (if your opponent obstinately refuses to resign), it is essential to be familiar with the correct procedure.

White	Black
1. Re8–f8	

Limiting the black king.

1. . . .	Kg5–g4
2. Ke1–e2	Kg4–g3
3. Ke2–e3	Kg3–g4
4. Rf8–f1	Kg4–g5

Both sides are playing the best moves.

5. Ke3–e4	Kg5–g6
6. Ke4–e5	Kg6–g7
7. Ke5–e6	Kg7–g6
8. Rf1–g1 ch.	

The king is now forced to the edge of the board. Note the position of the white king at the precise moment of the check: it is directly opposite the black king, thereby controlling the three squares between them that would otherwise have been open to the fugitive. The black king is now confined to the h file. White aims to set up the same position to deliver checkmate.

8. . . .	Kg6–h5
9. Ke6–f5	Kh5–h4

10. Rg1–g8	Kh4–h3
11. Kf5–f4	Kh3–h2
12. Kf4–f3	Kh2–h1
13. Kf3–f2	Kh1–h2

The black king is forced to face the white king: the curtain falls.

14. Rg8–h8 mate

The maximum number of moves required for this type of ending is seventeen – and this only in extreme cases.

King and two Rooks v. King
This is a very easy ending, the two rooks being moved rank by rank or file by file, to the edge of the board where the lone king is checkmated.

Place the white king on e1, the two white rooks on a1 and h1, and the black king on e4. White mates in eight moves by:

1. Ra1–a3 (Rh1–h3 also forces mate in eight), Ke4–f4; 2. Rh1–h4 ch., Kf4–g5; 3. Rh4–b4, Kg5–f5; 4. Ra3–a5 ch., Kf5–e6; 5. Rb4–b6 ch., Ke6–d7; 6. Ra5–a7 ch., Kd7–c8; 7. Ra7–h7, Kc8–d8; 8. Rb6–b8 mate.

King and two Bishops v. King
The ending with king and two bishops embraces the same idea of driving the lone king to the edge of the board, the pieces working in conjunction to cut-off the escape squares (or flight squares, as they are more commonly called). The king must be mated on a corner square, and in this respect the mate differs from the endings with queen and rook given above.

King, Bishop and Knight v. King

The ending with king, bishop and knight against bare king is conducted in the same manner as the ending with the two bishops, except that the victim must be mated on a corner square of the same colour as that on which the bishop stands.

Most elementary text-books on chess give pages of analysis on these two endings which serve only to bewilder the student. Many experienced players are unable to force the mate with bishop and knight. And, indeed, why worry? In my experience I have never played or seen played an ending of this nature. Archaic instruction is almost always a forerunner of boredom and disinterest.

King and Pawn Endings

When the tumult of the middle game has subsided into the comparative quiet of the end game, it is usual for each side to be left with a few pawns and perhaps a piece or two. With only a handful of men remaining it is easier to calculate with precision the best line of play – indeed, the end game of chess is a fine art, and there are many books devoted to this subject alone.

With only a limited force available, it is unlikely that either king is in danger of being mated. The play is therefore concentrated on the task of queening (promoting) pawns – which does not mean to say that either player should lose sight of mating possibilities.

As soon as one side succeeds in promoting a pawn, he will obviously have a decided, if not decisive advantage, and can then turn his attention to destroying the enemy force preparatory to the final checkmate.

On a crowded board the likelihood of a pawn surviving the hazardous march from the second to the eighth rank is remote; but as the forces decrease its power augments. It will be seen, therefore, that in the end game the pawn takes on a new importance, since the longer it survives the greater are its chances of eventual promotion.

To understand even the simplest end games, it is necessary to study the movements of the pawn in conjunction with the movements of the friendly king vis-à-vis the hostile king.

Look at the diagram (11). Here are four simple examples of king and pawn endings.

DIAGRAM 11

BLACK

WHITE

PAWN – PLAY

In (a), Black to move is a draw, since the king is stalemated. White, to move, wins, however. 1. Kb6–c6, Kb8–a7 (the only move); 2. Kc6–c7 (still guarding the pawn and preventing Black returning to the promotion square), Ka7–a6; 3. Pb7–b8(Q) and White mates in two more moves.

In (b), Black to move is a draw (stalemate). If White to move, he is in a quandary. The only square to which he can play the king and still guard the pawn (g6) leaves the black king in stalemate, whilst any other king move permits Black to capture the pawn. From which we derive the important precept that if, in a king and rook's pawn v. king ending, the solitary king can reach the queening square before the pawn, the game is drawn.

The difference between 11 (a) and 11 (b) will now be apparent. In (a) the white king penetrates by forcing the black king out on the opposite file; whereas in (b) he is not able to do this.

In (c) the king is unable to capture either pawn without permitting the other to queen. For example, 1. Kb2–c3, Pa4–a3; 2. Kc3xc4, Pa3–a2 and queens (promotes to queen) next move. The white king can only shuffle impotently between b2 and b1 until the black king arrives on the scene to force the issue. Black loses both pawns in an attempt to promote one without assistance:

1. Kb2–b1, Pc4–c3; 2. Kb1–c2, Pa4–a3; 3. Kc2xc3, Pa3–a2; 4. Kc3–b2.

In (d) White can again do nothing but move his king around until the black king arrives. If he captures the unprotected pawn he cannot stop the other one queening.

Promotion Square

A simple rule for determining whether a pawn, advancing alone to promotion, can be captured by the king before it reaches the queening square, is illustrated in diagram 12.

Imagine a square with one side embracing the path from pawn to queening square. If the black king can move inside this square he can capture the pawn. In the diagram, Black, with the move, draws by playing Kb3–c3 or c4. White, with the move, wins by Ph3–h4, and the pawn cannot be stopped. If the pawn were at h2, White

would still win by virtue of the initial double pawn move
1. Ph2–h4. This rule only applies to a pawn advancing
alone: if the White king or other man can in any way
influence the play, the formula does not apply.

DIAGRAM 12
BLACK

WHITE
THE QUEENING SQUARE

Conclusion

You should now be possessed of a reasonable grasp of
the elementary principles of the game. In order that you
may not become over-wearied with theory we shall
proceed to play over a short game or two, assessing the
value of each move as we go.

Before passing on, however, try the following brief test
based on the points we have examined (answers on page
44):

(1) Place WK on a8, WN on e3; BK on h6, BQ on h2,
BB on b8. Black plays Bb8–a7 attacking the knight and

threatening Qh2–b8 mate. What result?

(2) In the king and queen ending given in this chapter, after Black played 6. . . . Kh6–h5, White mated by 7. Qg8–g5. Can you see any alternative mates for White in this position (one move)?

(3) Place WK on a1, WP on a4; BK on f5. Can Black, to move, prevent the WP queening?

(4) Place WK on d6, WR on d1; BK on e8. White to play. Mate in how many moves?

(5) Place WK on h5, WP on f7; BK on h7. White to play. What result?

(6) Place WK on b5, WP on b6; BK on b8. (i) White to move – what result? (ii) Black to move – what result?

Solution to Test (Chapter 2)

(1) Draw. White can play Ne3–g4 ch.! forking king and queen, thus leaving both sides with insufficient mating force. If White plays Ka8xa7?, Black plays simply Qh2–f2 pinning the knight, capturing it next move and winning easily with king and queen against king.

(2) Qg8–h8 or g7 – here the queen, notice, is only exercising her powers as a rook.

(3) Yes, by Kf5–e6, e5 or e4.

(4) Two: 1. Rd1–f1!, Ke8–d8; 2. Rf1–f8 mate.

(5) White wins: 1. Pf7–f8(R) etc. Not 1. Pf7–f8(Q) stalemate, or 1. Pf7–f8(B) or (N) with insufficient mating force. Black to play draws by Kh7–g7 winning the pawn.

(6) Draw in each case. (i) 1. Kb5–a6, Kb8–a8 (not 1. . . . Kb8–c8?; 2. Ka6–a7); 2. Pb6–b7 ch., Ka8–b8; and White must now give up the pawn or stalemate the black king. (ii) 1. . . . Kb8–b7! and White can do nothing except move about on the fifth rank as Black alternates between b8 and b7. If the white king tries to penetrate the sequel is as in (i). Note that 1. . . . Kb8–a8 (or c8) would be fatal: 2. Kb5–a6 (or c6), Ka8–b8; 3. Pb6–b7 wins (see diagram

11 (a)). On examination it will be seen that if one side can play a pawn to the seventh rank in this type of ending *without giving check,* and provided that the pawn is not an outside pawn, he will win.

3

EXAMPLES OF PLAY

The object of the game, we know, is to checkmate the opposing king. Since a direct assault is not always possible (and might result in placing one's own king in jeopardy) other, more immediate targets, must be found.

Three factors dominate the play:

  (i) Time – represented by the moves of the men.

 (ii) Force – represented by the powers of the men.

(iii) Space – represented by the territory controlled by the men.

A gain in time (or "tempo" as it is called), by forcing your opponent to waste moves, permits you to marshal your forces effectively and swiftly.

A gain in force by, say, capturing an enemy rook for bishop or a knight (known as "winning the exchange") is clearly advantageous.

A gain in space – extending your territorial control, thereby achieving greater manoeuvrability for your pieces – is again an obvious advantage.

Bearing these three points in mind, in addition to the ultimate aim of mating the opposing king, every move in a game should be made to some purpose.

If you have no plan, and aimlessly shift men around as the fancy takes you, you will rarely hold out for longer than a dozen or so moves. Better – far better – to have a bad plan than to have no plan at all. Which does not mean that a course of action, once formulated, should be adhered to obstinately; but rather that it should be modified or recast if necessary to meet changing conditions.

Remember, therefore, to play with a purpose at all times.

In chess, as in war, movements are governed by two determining factors – strategy and tactics. Strategy can be said to consist of the spade-work; tactics, which implements strategy, the point-to-point struggle.

Some players prefer the subtleties of finer strategy, others the exhilarating rough-and-tumble of tactical play; it is this distinction which to a greater or lesser degree determines a player's style.

So much for theory, and we are now ready to play over an actual game. The men are set up as in diagram 5, page 19 (black square left-hand corner!) and White moves first.

From hereon the short algebraic will be used. In this notation, the square from which a man moves is omitted, as is the dash. Thus Bf1–e2 is recorded simply as Be2. Sometimes ambiguity can arise. Look back at diagram 9. Assume White captures the black knight at b3 with the rook at b4. Rxb4 is not good enough because it is not clear which rook is taking the knight. In situations like this, either the rank (in this case) or the file on which the piece to be moved stands is given immediately after the initial letter. So the move would be written R4xb3. Similarly, if Black moves the knight e6 to d4, the move would be Ned4 since the knight at b3 could also move there. There is one other refinement: the pawn is not identified (which is itself an identification). Thus g2–g4 becomes simply g4. Where a pawn makes a capture, the file on which the pawn stands is given first; thus Pd5xe6 is rendered as dxe6, or sometimes simply xe6. Notice that no ambiguity is possible in the case of pawn moves.

White	Black
1. e4	

An excellent move. Note that the king's bishop and the queen are now free (in the initial position only the pawns and the knights are able to move). This pawn advance also strikes at the centre, which is the most important area of the board and the focus of all opening play.

1. . . .   e5

The same. One of Black's best replies. Clearly it achieves the same as White's move. Note that now neither of these pawns can move.

2. Nf3

The king's knight is brought into play. It attacks the black pawn and is therefore an aggressive move. It also attacks the square d4.

2. . . .   Nc6

Obvious and best. The pawn is now guarded, and the knight counter attacks square d4. It will be observed that the game to this point has revolved round the four centre squares. The struggle for these squares, control of which always yields the superior game, motivates most opening manoeuvres.

3. a4

A very weak move indeed: it demonstrates White has no plan. It does not serve a single useful function, being far removed from the central loci. White has dissipated the advantage of the extra move.

3. . . .   **Nf6**

A good move, it continues the assault on the centre, attacking White's KP.

4. Qe2

Bad. Although this move protects the threatened pawn, it hinders the development of the king's bishop. Bd3 in this position would have been no better, since then the queen's pawn would have been unable to move and White would have experienced difficulty in getting the queen's bishop out. Nc3 was correct.

4. . . .   **Bc5**

Another good move which develops a piece and attacks the square d4.

5. g3

White sees that he is unable to develop the bishop on the long diagonal, and seeks to bring it into play via g2.

5. . . .   **d6**

Black's QB is now able to come into the game.

6. Bg2

The bishop is now said to be "fianchettoed" in the jargon of the chess-player. In the old-time game, before the introduction of the double pawn move, it was usual to develop the bishops in this manner, since the centre pawns, only capable of moving one square at a time, would free one bishop only to block the other.

White could not, of course, play 6. Bh3 here, as the piece would then have been undefended, permitting Black to play Bxh3, winning a clear piece for nothing.

6. . . .   0–0

Castles. The black king is now in comparative safety, and the rook is brought into the game.

Up to here Black's moves have been an example of model play. At some points he has had the choice of several good moves, whilst other moves could have been transposed, but his play could hardly have been improved upon.

The position in diagram 13 has now been reached. Check this with your board to ensure that the two agree. A quick assessment of the game as it stands reveals that White has decidedly the worst of it. The KB is doing nothing, the queen is no better placed at e2 than at d1; and the a-pawn, a waif in the wilderness, has achieved nothing by its inconsequential advance.

Black on the other hand has his men posted to some purpose. His development (i.e., the bringing of his pieces into play) is almost complete, when he will be ready to embark on an attack. The contest may now be said to be entering the middle game. There are three recognized phases in a game of chess, the opening, middle game and end game. There is no strict dividing line between them, the opening being understood to consist of the developing moves of each side, the middle game the main struggle,

the end game when the majority of the pieces are off the
board and the kings and pawns come into their own. We
shall study each of these phases separately in ensuing
chapters.

DIAGRAM 13

POSITION AFTER BLACK'S 6TH MOVE

7. Qb5

Another bad move which threatens nothing; the black
bishop, knight and knight's pawn are all protected and the
KP is now unguarded. White should have again played
Nc3.

7. . . .   Nb4!

A very strong move, hence the exclamation mark.

Black now threatens to play Nxc2 ch., forking the king and the rook, with considerable material gain.

8. Na3

This guards the bishop's pawn, which would now make the exchange unfavourable to Black. White could also have played Kd1, but then the KBP would have been undefended, and, more important still, White would have forfeited the right to castle. c3 attacking the knight would also have been no good, since Black could still have continued Nc2 ch. winning the exchange at least. Qc4 would have allowed Black to continue Be6! attacking the queen and thereby gaining a "tempo".

8. ...   Bd7

The white queen is attacked.

9. Qc4

Note carefully that if, in this position, White had played instead Qxb7, Black would have replied Rb8! and the queen is without a flight square. White would then have had nothing better than to give up the queen for the rook.

9. ...   Be6
Again attacking the queen.

10. Qc3

Observe how an early foray with the queen is quickly punished. It is rarely advisable to bring the major pieces into the middle of the board at the beginning of a game, since they can be constantly harassed by the minor enemy pieces and much time is lost in the process. (The bishops and knights are known as the "minor" pieces, the rooks and queens as "major" pieces.) This move turns out to be very bad, as will be seen. Correct was Qe2.

10. . . .   Nxe4

The queen is trapped. 10. . . . Bxf2 ch. would also have been playable here, but after 11. Kd1 (not 11. Kxf2, Nxe4 ch. forking king and queen), Black cannot win the queen since after 11. . . . Nxe4; White can reply 12. Qxb4, the black bishop no longer defending this piece. Consequently the text move is much stronger.

11. d4

White opens the game – too late.

11. . . .   exd4

There is no hurry to take the queen off – she is still not able to escape. Note that the king's file is now open for Black's rook.

12. Nxd4   Nxc3
13. bxc3

As the result of this move White has what is known as "doubled pawns" – two pawns on the same file. The a-pawn is now isolated, and is called an "isolated pawn". Both these are weaknesses which we shall examine at a later stage; White's game is lost anyway.

13. . . .   Re8
14. cxb4

Ignoring the "discovered check" which is threatened by Black moving the QB, thereby exposing the white king to attack from the rook. Black has time to spare however, and first takes his piece back

14. . . .   Bxd4

Attacking the QR. c3 is no defence for White, as Black would play simply Bxc3 ch., forking king and rook.

15. Rb1

Now Black can play to win material by Ba2 dis. ch., when White, who must first deal with the check, will lose his rook. Observe the immense power of a discovered check – the bishop can go anywhere on the board without fear of capture, because White must first attend to the attack on his king.

15. . . .   Bc3 ch.

Not the best. Black does not take full advantage of the position in which there are several good continuations. He is so heavily up in material however – a queen and a pawn for a knight – that it matters little.

16. Kf1

Escaping from the discovered check, but Kd1 would have been better.

16. . . .   Bc4 ch.

Decisive.

17. Kg1

Not Nxc4, Re1 mate! Black sacrifices the bishop in order to clear the file for the rook. It may be argued that such an offer hardly constitutes a sacrifice. Certainly it is not a sacrifice in the true sense, but chess terminology rules that it shall be so described, so there it is.

The sacrifice is one of the keenest sources of delight to the chess-player, the apparent surrender of force creating a whimsical effect which is at once self-satisfying and artistic. This is an example of a tactical sacrifice – by far the most common. The strategical sacrifice – the relinquishing of a pawn or a piece in order to gain time or space, particularly in the opening – is more common among stronger players as it requires sound judgment.

17. . . .   **Re1 ch.**
18. Bf1

The only move.

18. . . .   **Rxf1 ch.**
19. Kg2

The king cannot, of course, take the rook since it is defended by the QB.

19. . . .   **Bd5 ch.**
20. Kh3?

20. Kxf1, Bxh1 was much better, but naturally not 20. f3, Rxf3 when Black would again be threatening a dangerous discovered check.

20. . . .   **Qd7 ch.**
21. Kh4

21. g4 would only have protracted the agony.

21. . . .   **Bf3**

Now mate cannot be avoided. It is often the quiet move
rather than the garish check that precedes the climax.

22. Kg5   **Qg4 mate**

Finis. See diagram 14.

DIAGRAM 14

FINAL POSITION

Observations

By normal standards this is a short game, the average
being around thirty-five moves. A long game will run to
sixty moves and more – occasionally into three figures.

There are a number of lessons to be learned from the play of both sides, but the main cause of White's collapse was his dilatory handling of the opening. It was evident almost from the outset that he had no plan of campaign.

Witness Black's handling of the game by comparison – a polished if not perfect performance.

  (i) He developed his pieces quickly.

 (ii) He took advantage of White's errors.

(iii) He wasted no time in side issues.

It is of particular interest to notice that Black succeeded in castling and bringing his king's rook into play, the uncastled white king offering a vulnerable target.

In the final position observe the confusion in the white ranks. The QB and KR are still "at home"; the QN is posted at the side of the board guarding a threat which for many moves has ceased to exist; the QR has been forced to waste a tempo to avoid the attack of a minor piece; and, of course, that unhappy pawn is still forlornly standing, without rhyme or reason, on a4. A sorry picture!

Three Brevities

The shortest game of chess possible is a brevity known as Fool's Mate. It runs to only two moves:

White	*Black*
1. f3	**e5**
2. g4	**Qh4 mate**

None of White's king's side pieces is able to interpose.

The term "Fool's Mate" is something of a misnomer, since in his early acquaintance with the game the beginner may easily overlook the vulnerability of his king, particularly when the attacking piece descends "from the blue".

On the other hand, a game concluded in four moves known as the "Scholar's Mate" is much more obvious. White wins this time:

White	Black
1. e4	e5
2. Bc4	Bc5
3. Qh5	Nf6
4. Qxf7 mate	

If Black had played Nf6 before he brought the bishop out all would have been well, as Qh5 could then have been met by Nxh5. But in any case Black had nothing to fear if he fathomed White's designs. For example, 3. . . . Qe7, defending both the threatened mate and the e-pawn was good since, as we have learned from the previous game, White will lose time parrying Black's imminent attacks on the wayward queen.

Variations and extensions of these two mating themes are often encountered. The f-pawn, against which the attack in Scholar's Mate is directed, is the weakest link in the initial position, for it is guarded only by the king. A further point in favour of castling: the rook is brought to the protection of this pawn.

Here is another short game with an attractive sacrifice:

White	Black
1. e4	e5
2. Nf3	d6
3. Bc4	h6
4. Nc3	Bg4

Pinning the knight.

5. Nxe5!

The surprise: White sacrifices the queen.

5. . . .   **Bxdl**

This loses, but after 5. . . . dxe4; 6. Qxg4, White has won a pawn and is ahead in development

6. Bxf7 ch.

That weak f-pawn again!

6. . . .   **Ke7**
7. Nd5 mate.

Before returning to the study of chess theory, the reader would do well to play over another game and endeavour to answer the questions posed.

Initial position again – black square left-hand corner – queens on the squares of their own colour.

White	*Black*
1. e4	**e5**
2. Bc4	

(a) Good or bad?

2. . . .   **Na6**

(b) Is this better than Nc6?

3.Nf3

The black pawn is now attacked and is said to be *en*

prise (Fr: 'in a position to be taken').

| 3. . . . | f6? |

It is a good general rule that this move is bad in the opening, seriously weakening the king's position.

4. Nxe5!

A tactical sacrifice.

| 4. . . . | fxe5 |

Black has nothing better.

| 5. Qh5 ch. | g6 |

(c) Why not 5. . . . Ke7?

6. Qxe5 ch.	Qe7
7. Qxh8	Qxe4 ch.
8. Be2	

(d) Why not Kd1 or Kf1?

| 8. . . . | Ne7 |

(e) What was White threatening?

| 9. d3 | Qxg2 |
| 10. Bh6 | |

Another sacrifice.

| 10. . . . | Qxh1 ch. |
| 11. Kd2 | d6 |

(f) Why cannot Black play Bxh6 ch.?

    12. Qxf8 ch.   **Kd7**
    13. Bg5

A strong move, as will be seen. The black knight is
twice attacked, and since it cannot be further protected by
another man, it must move or be captured.

    13. . . .   **Nf5**

(g) Why not Nc6?

    14. Qf7 ch.   **Kc6**
    15. Nc3!

Another good sacrifice. The rook is *en prise* to the black
queen.

    15. . . .   **Qg2**

The only move. Black must keep on the diagonal to
prevent the bishop check. If 15. . . . Qxa1? there would
follow 16. Bf3 ch., when Black would be mated in three
moves at most. How? (h).

    16. Rg1!

A pretty move. The QB is attacked by the black queen,
so White promptly offers the rook again, hoping to decoy
the queen off the vital diagonal.

    16. . . .   **Qxf2**

Now the white KB is pinned.

17. Rf1

(i) If 17. Be3, attacking the queen and guarding the rook, how would Black have continued?

17. . . .   Qg2
18. Kd1

(j) Why?

18. . . .   d5

Clearly not 18. . . . Ne3 ch?; 19. Bxe3. Or 18. . . . Kb6; 19. Qb3 ch. Another possible line is 18. . . . Nd4; 19. Qc4 ch., Nc5 (19. . . . Kd7?; 20. Rf7 ch., Ke8; 21. Re7 ch., Kf8; 22. Qf7 mate; or 21. . . . Kd8, Qg8 mate.) 20. Bf3 ch! – yet another sacrifice – Nxf3; 21. Qb5 mate.

19. Nxd5

(k) Why not still 19. Bf3?

19. . . .   Nc5

(1) Why not 19. . . . Qxd5?

20. Qxc7 ch.

White, offering a further knight, wins the queen at last.

20. . . .   Kxd5

(m) Can Black play 20. . . . Kb5, declining the tainted gift?

21. Bf3 ch.

White misses a conclusive finish: 21. Rxf5 ch., B(or P)xf5; 22. c4 ch., Kd4; (22. . . . Ke6? 23. Qe7 mate) 23. Qd6 ch., Qd5; 24. Qxd5 mate.

21. . . .	**Qxf3 ch.**
22. Rxf3	**Resigns**

Black has two knights for a queen and a pawn. He has no chance of redressing the balance, and his king is in the centre of the board open to continuous attack. Under the circumstances, a graceful surrender is the best course.

Observations

This is the kind of punishment that the student must expect to receive from the strong player. A wasted knight move, an injudicious pawn advance and it was virtually all over.

White sacrified continually throughout the game and yet won with ease. Why? Because on each occasion he correctly assessed the relative values of the men engaged, and played accordingly.

Sacrifices of this nature have to be very carefully calculated, however, since a single slip in analysis would prove disastrous.

For this reason the student is advised not to give up voluntarily even a pawn unless he can foresee the consequences. As you progress you will often be able to sense a sacrifice, but insight of this nature comes only with practice.

All sacrifices should be treated on their merits alone. Regrettably, this seemingly trite advice is rarely followed. Beginners tend to fall into two classes; those who grab everything on the principle that they then have the superior force and it is incumbent upon the opponent to maintain the initiative; and those who never accept anything on the principle that if a man is offered it must be a trap.

If you see no objection to accepting a proffered piece, do not hestitate. An apparent sacrifice is often an oversight: the player has simply put or left a man *en prise*.

Solutions to Test – Chapter 3

(a) Good, since it develops a piece, prevents Black playing d5, and attacks the weak f-pawn. The usual rule, and a good one to stick to when learning the game, is "knights and bishops out first".

(b) No. It is away from the centre of the board. The knight on a6 controls four unimportant squares – exactly half the number of squares it would control on c6.

(c) Because of Qxe5 checkmate!

(d) Because the bishop is *en prise*.

(e) 9. Qxg8.

(f) Because the bishop is pinned by the white queen.

(g) Because of Bg4 mate.

(h) (1) 16. . . . d5; 17. Qxd5 ch., Kb6; 18. Qb5 or Na4 mate.

(2) 16. . . . Kc5; 17. Qc4 (or d5) ch., K moves; 18. Qb5 mate.

(3) 16. . . , Kb6; 17. Qb3 ch., Nb4; (17. . . . Ka5; 18. Qb5 mate) 18. Qxb4 ch., Ka6; 19. Qb5 mate.

(i) 17. . . . Qxe3 ch. (not 17. . . . Nxe3? 18. Qxf2); 18. Kd1, Qxg1 ch.; and Black wins easily, being a R, N and P ahead. This move (17. Be3) would have been a bad blunder on White's part.

(j) To un-pin the bishop. The move threatens Bf3 ch., winning the queen. Note that the white bishop at g5 is now *en prise*. White forced Black to capture the f-pawn, a sacrifice that permitted the white rook to make use of the open file to guard f3 so that the bishop can check.

(k) Because of 18. . . . Qxf1 ch.

(l) Because of 20. Bf3, and the queen is pinned and lost.

(m) No; Black would then be mated by 21. a4 ch., Ka6; 22. Nb4. Or 21. . . . Nxa4; 22. Qc4 ch., Ka5; 23. b4 mate; If 21. . . . Kxa4, White can mate in several ways: 22. Nc3 ch. followed by 23. Rf4 ch.; or 22. b3 ch. followed by 23. Bc1 ch. etc.

4

POWERS OF THE
CHESSMEN

If the previous chapters have been followed carefully, the reader should now have a good idea of how to play chess. Should he still be uncertain on any point he would be well advised to turn back here and dispel any doubts before proceeding further.

The last chapter was devoted to actual games, as a means of breaking the inevitable boredom that the study of page upon page of theory engenders; but now it is necessary to return to the elements of play.

As has been seen, the functions and values of the chessmen vary from stage to stage individually, collectively and relatively.

It is possible to generalise on the powers and limitations of the various men throughout the game, and to lay down broad principles for handling them.

It will be as well to repeat here that the three phases through which a game can pass are:

(a) The opening – development of the pieces.

(b) The middle game – the main struggle.

(c) The end game – the fight for pawn-promotion.

A game can be concluded in the opening or the middle game without ever reaching the end game (as in the illustrative examples in Chapter 3), the three divisions having no relation to the duration of a game; that is to say, the end game is not the last moves of any chess game, but specifically that field of play in which the majority of the pieces are off the board and the kings and pawns dominate the play.

Bearing this in mind, let us examine the pieces individually under these three headings.

1. The Opening

(a) King

The king should be kept closely guarded in the opening, when a surprise attack is always a danger. Early castling is advisable, and in this respect the K-side is to be preferred to the queen's, since after the latter the QRP is unprotected.

(b) Queen

It is inadvisable to move the queen beyond the third rank where she is prone to attack from the light enemy forces. Contravention of this maxim may result in loss of time occasioned by the queen having to seek sanctuary.

(c) Rook

The rooks should be united (i.e., one guarding the other) as soon as possible. Castling is a means of achieving this aim.

Rooks should be retained on the back rank, preferably on open files.

(d) Bishop

The bishops should be developed early in the game. The best squares for posting the white bishops (corresponding squares for the black bishop) are (1) c4/f4; (2) b5/g5 if pinning an enemy knight; (3) b2/g2 – the fianchetto; (4) d2/e2; (5) d3/e3 if here they do not block the advance of their respective centre pawns.

(e) Knight

Knights are employed to their best advantage in the opening. They should be developed towards the centre of the board unless there are good tactical reasons for not doing so.

(f) Pawn

The first thing to remember about the pawn move – and this applies to all stages of the game – is that, unlike the pieces, it may not be retraced. In other words, a minor rubicon is crossed every time a pawn is moved; therefore all pawn moves should be made only after careful deliberation. Ask yourself: "If I advance this pawn, am I likely to regret it at a later stage?"

A pawn advance on one or more of the four central files is normal and necessary in the opening. A single exception may be noted: f3 (f6) is almost invariably bad as it seriously weakens the king's position and takes away the best square for the king's knight.

A knight's pawn may be moved a single square to permit the development of a bishop; a rook's pawn a single square to prevent the pinning of a knight by a hostile bishop. But a good rule is: if in doubt, don't move a pawn.

2. The Middle Game
(a) King

As in the opening, the king must be protected against

attack. Towards the end of the middle game with most of the pieces off the board, an uncastled king which is required for active service is best advanced to the second rank rather than relegated to a wing position by the no-longer useful castling.

(b) Queen

The queen is a real power, and can often be man-oeuvred to attack two undefended units simultaneously, thereby winning one of them. The queen should avoid picking up stray pawns if they beguile her from the scene of activities. On the other hand, a pawn safely won is a clear advantage.

This is a further point on which the expert can be distinguished from the ordinary player – he knows which pawn can be safely captured and which pawn should be left alone.

(c) Rook

The rooks are best placed on the four centre files, particularly if any should be "open" (a file is said to be open if there are no friendly pawns on it). Doubled rooks (one behind the other) are very strong on an open file.

A rook (or better still, doubled rooks) on the seventh rank is something to be played for, as here the major pieces are immune from pawn attack, and assume the role of "cats among the pigeons".

Rooks are especially vulnerable to attack from the bishops – particularly if the latter are working in conjunction: therefore they should, if possible, be confined to the first two ranks unless an occupation of the seventh is feasible.

(d) Bishop

The bishops are the real workers – they never relax

their activities throughout the game.

They are dangerous attacking pieces, but operate best, like the rooks, from a distance where they are less open to attack themselves.

A common task of the bishop is to pin potentially active hostile knights.

As has been observed, the bishop, like the rook and the queen, operates to greater advantage on an open board.

The efficacy of the bishops depends on free diagonals, therefore avoid curtailing their range by obstructive pawn moves.

(e) Knight

Knights are quite at home in the middle game, and are best posted on advanced squares free from pawn attack.

They are economical in defence, being capable of holding up an assault by considerably superior forces on the king; and very effective in attack, the sacrifice of a knight for a pawn often completely destroying an otherwise impregnable position.

Knights are least effective when guarding one another, since, if both are attacked by a piece, neither can move without loss of the other. They are most effective when working in conjunction on opposite-coloured squares.

(f) Pawn

The pawns are as important in the middle game as they are in the other stages.

In defence, they present a united front to direct onslaught; the more they are moved the weaker they become as a body creating "holes", or undefended squares, for occupation by enemy pieces.

In attack, the pawns are the battering-rams used to breach the enemy position. A spearhead of pawns, supported by pieces, advancing on a king position stands an infinitely greater chance of success than an attack by pieces alone.

Pawns are well-employed defending pieces from attack by hostile pieces, and they are also the best men with which to attack hostile pieces because of their relatively inferior value.

It must be kept in mind throughout the middle game that all pawns are potential queens. Try to picture the skeleton when the meat is off, and play for a favourable end game position before forcing the exchange of too many pieces.

3. The End Game
(a) King

In the ending the king assumes the role of attacker, and his transitory function is to assist in pawn-promotion.

The versatility of the king at close range allows him to penetrate weak pawn structures.

Too often, when the end game is reached, players continue to manoeuvre their few remaining pieces instead of bringing the kings forward.

If the opposing forces still contain three or more pieces, an early advance of the king is likely to prove an embarrassment.

(b) Queen

With the reduction in forces, the queen's power augments. If in a bad position in the middle game, the retention of the queen will at least offer chances of a "perpetual" in the ending, for a lone queen can often force the draw in this manner.

(c) Rook

The rooks, since they are generally the last pieces to go into action in a game, are most commonly met with in end games; king, rook and pawns versus king, rook and pawns being by far the most frequent.

A book could well be written on the functions of this piece in the ending alone, but briefly the work of the rook is confined to three fields:

  (i) Restricting the movements of the hostile king.
  (ii) "Mopping-up" and obstructing the advance of hostile pawns.
  (iii) Protecting friendly pawns advancing to promotion.

A rook on the seventh rank – particularly if the enemy king is still on the eighth – is almost always strong, as in the middle game.

Two rooks on the seventh with the enemy king on the eighth usually draws by perpetual check against a similar piece-force, even if a pawn or two down.

Whereas an extra pawn in a king and pawn end game is usually sufficient to win, with rooks on the board the chances favour a draw. Therefore if a pawn or more down in the ending, endeavour to retain a rook on the board.

All these factors should be borne in mind when the middle game is drawing to a close.

(d) Bishop

A paramount maxim to remember here is that if each side is left with a bishop and pawns, and the two bishops are on opposite coloured squares, the game is nearly always drawn, even if one side is a pawn or even two pawns ahead.

If a disadvantageous end game is foreshadowed, play to obtain bishops of opposite colours.

With bishops on squares of the same colour, however, even a small advantage on one side is often sufficient to win.

The reason for this is that, with bishops of opposite colours, the play of each side tends to be canalised onto the squares of the same colour as the respective bishops, leaving one party playing on the black squares and the other party operating on the white, thereby creating a deadlock. With bishops operating on the same coloured squares, force will be met by force, and an impasse is less likely to occur.

Another important fact to remember in the ending is that K, B and RP versus bare K is a draw where the bishop stands on a square the opposite colour to the pawn's promotion square; always provided that the solitary king can get in front of the advancing pawn. As in K and RP versus K, the superior force is compelled to surrender the pawn (leaving insufficient mating force) or give stalemate. With a bishop on the same-colour square as the promotion square, the stronger side always wins in this type of ending.

Bishops can be employed to good purpose preventing hostile pawn advances. For example, a white bishop on f1 prevents the advance of any black pawn in a chain of squares extending from f2 to e3, d4, c5 and b6. This is an elaborate case, but it demonstrates the power of the bishop in the end game.

If, in an ending, you are left with a bishop and pawns, the pawns should be advanced to squares of the *opposite* colour to that on which the bishop stands.

This may appear strange, since the bishop cannot then guard the pawns, but this drawback is outweighed by the bishop's greatly increased mobility, and the elimination of duplicated square control. It is quite a common sight to see a bishop reduced to the role of a pawn when the men stand on the squares of one colour.

(e) Knight

In the ending the powers of the knight are limited,

owing to the comparative impotence of its march on a free board.

A player left with knight and pawns against a bishop and pawn should, if possible, force off by exchanges the pawns on one side of the board, as knight is seriously handicapped in having to watch both wings. The converse, of course, holds good – if left with a bishop and pawns against a knight and pawns, essay to keep pawns on both wings, on which the bishop, with its greater powers, is able to operate simultaneously.

(f) Pawn

When one talks of the end game one is really discussing pawns, and their handling is therefore of the utmost importance.

Their play is examined at length in the chapter on the end game; it suffices here to quote a few general rules.

When there is a choice of pawn moves in the ending, the one that is farthest from the scene of operations (usually centred around the kings) should be made.

Remember always that a rook's pawn is insufficient to win, other things being equal, therefore pawn exchanges must be planned accordingly.

The advance of a pawn can be arrested by the sacrifice of a piece if necessary, a device which should not be overlooked.

In the ending, the remote wing pawns play their part, the centre struggle no longer dominating the game. A king cannot possibly stop two pawns, one advancing on each wing, but he can successfully blockade two centre pawns advancing together.

As with the pieces, a cautionary eye must be kept on the pawns in the middle game, in order that they may be deployed to the best advantage when the final phase is reached.

Combinations

So much for the general manipulation of the men at the various stages. Let us now see how they can combine effectively. The joint action of two or more men, working to achieve a desired object – to checkmate the opposing king, or capture material – is known as a combination; a sound combination if its purpose cannot be resisted, an unsound combination if there exists a plausible defence. Combinations are often initialled by a sacrifice.

There are a number of standard mates which keep occurring in one form or another, the dispersal of the majority of the men being purely incidental to the position.

A player should be able to recognise these positions at once, regardless of the camouflage concealing them.

The following examples are all quite common in practice, and cover the majority of actual mating attacks in the middle game. Be on guard against any and every similar position, however secure it may appear, for a deflective sacrifice, that cannot be declined, may be the prelude to catastrophe.

Mating Combinations

(a) A variation of Fool's Mate, involving the sacrifice of a piece, is commonly encountered in play. It can occur in the opening: 1. f4, e5; 2. fxe5, d6; 3. exd6, Bxd6; 4. Nc3?, Qh4 ch.; 5. g3, Qxg3 ch.; 6. hxg3, Bxg3 mate (diagram 15).

(b) A typical middle game sacrifice is to take the h-pawn with a bishop when the enemy king has castled on the king's side. A conclusive combination is often possible. In the diagram (16) White wins by 1. Bxh7 ch., Kxh7?; 2. Qh5 ch., Kg8; 3. Ng5, Rfe8; 4. Qh7 ch., Kf8; 5. Qh8 mate.

(c) After the sacrifice of a bishop for the h-pawn, the

DIAGRAM 15   **DIAGRAM 16**

EXAMPLE A   EXAMPLE B

most common mating attack begins with the sacrifice of a bishop for the f-pawn against an unmoved king. Diagram 17 shows a typical example. White wins by 1. Bxf7 ch., Kxf7; 2. Ne5 dbl. ch. (that fearsome double check again! – the king must move), Ke6; (if 2. . . . Ke8; 3. Qh5 ch. and mate in two; if 2. . . . Ke7; 3. Nd5 ch.) 3. Qg4 ch., Kxe5 (again . . . . Ke7; 4. Nd5 ch.); 4. Qf4 ch., Kd4 (or 4. . . . Ke6; 5. Qf5 ch. with mate to follow); 5. Be3 mate. The forced march of the black king into the centre of the board is a feature of this type of attack.

(d) Mate on the back rank by a rook or the queen is common if the pawns in front of the king have not been moved. In diagram 18 White wins by: 1. Re8 ch., Rxe8; 2. Rxe8 ch., Rxe8; 3. Qxe8 mate. Always be alert to this possibility: decoy sacrifices are common.

(e) An ingenious attack, involving a queen sacrifice on the penultimate move, is known as Philidor's Legacy,

DIAGRAM 17   **DIAGRAM 18**

EXAMPLE C   EXAMPLE D

after a famous French player (diagram 19). White forces
mate in five moves: 1. Qc4 ch., Kh8; (if 1. . . . Kf8;
2. Qf7 mate) 2. Nf7 ch., Kg8; 3. Nh6 dbl. ch., Kh8

DIAGRAM 19   **DIAGRAM 20**

EXAMPLE E   EXAMPLE F

(otherwise mate as above: note once again the power of the double check which White here uses to manoeuvre the knight to the desired square); 4. Qg8 ch., Rxg8 (the king cannot capture as the knight guards the queen); 5. Nf7 mate.

(f) Philidor's Legacy demonstrates what is commonly known as a "smothered mate". The description is a good one; all the escape squares for the king being occupied by friendly (?) pieces who stifle the luckless monarch. Smothered mate can only be given by a knight, and is not uncommonly preceded by a sacrifice, as in the previous example. This device can occur in the opening: 1. e4, e5; 2. Ne2, Nc6; 3. Nbc3, Nd4; 4. g3, Nf3 mate (diagram 20).

(g) A position to be played for if your opponent has castled on the queen's side (diagram 21). White wins quickly by 1. Qxc6 ch., bxc6; 2. Ba6 mate. Note the power of the two bishops working together.

DIAGRAM 21   DIAGRAM 22

EXAMPLE G   EXAMPLE H

(h) A king behind a fianchettoed position from which the bishop has departed is very weak if the queens are still on the board, particularly if the other player has retained the bishop on the same coloured squares as the departed bishop, and/or a knight. Examples of this type are common, the strategy being to attack the weak squares in the king's field. In diagram 22 White wins by 1. Qh6 (threatening mate on the move), Bf8; 2. Ne7 ch., Bxe7; 3. Qg7 mate. In this type of position a pawn at f6 is often as good as a bishop; and with a queen established at h6, Nf6 ch. followed by Qxh7 mate is also a common finale.

(i) A device against a fianchettoed position (normally difficult to attack: diagram 23). White mates in four by 1. Nf6 ch., Bxf6; 2. Rxe8 ch., Kg7; 3. Bf8 ch., K moves; 4. Bh6 mate. If 1. . . . Kh8; 2. Rxe8 ch., Bf8; 3. Bxf8 and mates next move.

DIAGRAM 23

EXAMPLE I

(j) Another mating position often reached when the

bishop has vacated the fianchetto (diagram 24). White mates in three by 1. Qxh7 ch., Kxh7; 2. Rh3 ch., Kg8; 3. Rh8 mate.

DIAGRAM 24

EXAMPLE J

(k) An end game attack on a castled king (diagram 25).

DIAGRAM 25

EXAMPLE K

White mates in three: 1. Re8 ch., Kh7; 2. Bf5 ch., g6; 3. Rh8 mate. The pawn move closes the line of one bishop only to open a line for the other. All Black's moves are forced.

(l) With the hostile king in the corner, a typical mating set-up starts with a queen sacrifice (diagram 26): 1. Qxh7 ch., Kxh7; Rh3 mate.

DIAGRAM 26

EXAMPLE L

(m) A less usual position, but nevertheless frequently occurring in one form or another (diagram 27). White wins by 1. Rxg7 ch., Rxg7; 2. Nf6 ch., Kh8; 3. Qh5 and mate is unavoidable. If 1. . . . Kh8; White can win in a number of ways, for example 2. Qg2, Be6; 3. Qg6 and mate next move. Black can prolong the agony by sacrificing the queen.

DIAGRAM 27

EXAMPLE M

Material-Winning Combinations

There exist a number of stereotyped combinations for winning material (i.e. gaining an enemy man or men for nothing, or for the loss of a weaker force) arising from certain positions that are met with time and again in one form or another.

A sound knowledge of these basic positions and how to exploit them will prove of inestimable value to the student.

Three good rules to observe in order to avoid loss of material are:

(1) Watch all checks.

(2) Watch all "discovered" attacks.

(3) Do not leave men undefended or insufficiently defended unless absolutely necessary.

(a) An attack on the king (a check) may often succeed in winning material out of hand:

(1) It may force the defender to interpose a stronger piece than the man checking, which then captures it.

(2) The checking piece may simultaneously attack an undefended man, or a more valuable man (a knight fork is a good example of this).

(3) The move may uncover ("discover") an attack on another man.

(4) If a piece on each side is attacked, and one can evade the attack by a checking move, then the other piece, still *en prise*, will fall.

(5) The skewer, illustrated in diagram 10 is yet another means of winning material in this fashion.

An example of (1) taken from play: 1. e4, c5; 2. Nf3, d6; 3. Nc3, Bg4; 4. h3, Bxf3; 5. Qxf3, Na6; 6. Bb5 ch., and the queen must interpose. To illustrate (2), another example from actual play: 1. d3, c6; 2. Nf3, e5; 3. Nxe5, Qa5 ch.; and the undefended knight is captured next move.

A trap in a well-known defence demonstrates the discovered attack (3): 1. e4, e6; 2. d4, d5; 3. e5, c5; 4. Nf3, Nc6; 5. c3, Qb6; 6. Bd3, cxd4; 7. cxd4, Nxd4; 8. Nxd4 – the trap is sprung – 8. . . . Qxd4?; 9. Bb5 ch., and the black queen is lost (diagram 28).

A game opening will serve to make (4) clear: 1. e4, c5; 2. Nf3, d6; 3. Bc4, Bg4; 4. Nc3, Nc6; 5. h3, Bh5; 6. g4 (attacking the bishop again), Na5 (attacking White's

DIAGRAM 28

FINAL POSITION

bishop); 7. Bb5 ch. winning a piece (diagram 29). These opening examples given to demonstrate elementary stratagems are not, of course, intended as patterns of model play.

DIAGRAM 29

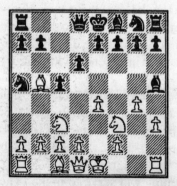

FINAL POSITION

(b) When two undefended men are attacked simultaneously, one is frequently lost. In the diagram (30), the rook threatens both the knight and the bishop and must win one of them.

(c) Underprotection. A common failing of inexperienced players is to use one man to perform two functions – for example, guarding two pieces. In the diagram (31), the black king is defending both the knight and the bishop. White wins a piece by: 1. Nxa1, Kxa1; 2. Kxc1.

(d) Two knights guarding one another are weak. In the diagram (32) the rook is attacking both knights. The white bishop is threatening to capture one of them, and Black must lose a piece.

(e) A similar type of manoeuvre to (a) is the threat of mate combined with an attack on an undefended man.

DIAGRAM 30

DIAGRAM 33

DIAGRAM 31

DIAGRAM 32

Such a position may occur early in the game. Examine diagram 33, a position which can arise from an opening called the Colle System: Black's previous move (b6) was bad, and now White threatens both Qh7 mate and Qxa8. The mate must be attended to, and the rook is consequently lost.

(f) The "discovered" attack almost always wins material: 1. e4, e5; 2. Nf3, Nc6; 3. Bc4, Nf6; 4. d3, Nh5?; 5. Nxe5 (discovering the queen attack on the unprotected knight), Nxe5; 6. Qxh5 and White has won a pawn.

(g) A similar device to (f) which also wins a pawn: 1. e4, e6; 2. d4, d5; 3. e5, c5; 4. c3, Nc6; 5. Bb5, Bd7; 6. Nf3?, Nxe5. And now if 7. Bxd7 ch., Nxd7; and if 7. Nxe5 (or dxe5), Bxb5.

This very common trap continues to net a large haul of victims (including quite experienced players) year after year. The diagram (34) gives the position after Black's 6th move.

DIAGRAM 34

(h) A common material-winning device, particularly in the opening, is the advance on a hemmed-in bishop: 1. e4, c5; 2. Nf3, Nc6, 3. Bc4, d6; 4. 0–0, a6; 5. Qe2?, b5; 6. Bd3 (or Bb3), c4; (diagram 35). White must give up the bishop for two pawns, an exchange we know to be unfavourable.

DIAGRAM 35

(i) A pinned man, being immobile, is particularly vulnerable to pawn attack. In the opening after, for example, 1. c4, e5; 2. Nc3, Nc6; 3. e3, Nf6; 4. d4, d6; 5. Qa4, Bf5? White wins a piece for a pawn by 6. d5 and Black's pinned knight must fall. The diagram (36) shows the position after White's final move.

(j) A king may be lured from the defence of a man by a check – very often by a sacrifice. This is also liable to occur in the opening. A good example is offered: 1. e4, c5; 2. Nf3, Nc6; 3. d4, cxd4; 4. Nxd4, Nf6; 5. Nc3, d6; 6. Bc4, g6; 7. Nxc6, bxc6; 8. e5, dxe5?; 9. Bxf7 ch. (see diagram 37). Now Black must take with the king leaving the queen undefended.

DIAGRAM 36

DIAGRAM 37   DIAGRAM 38

(k) A "forced" move, that is to say a move that must be made either to save the game or as a matter of legality, may frequently concede material. Diagram 38 shows a common strategm. White plays here Bh6, threatening Qxg7 mate. The bishop cannot be taken as the g-pawn is pinned, and g5 would allow mate in two by Qxg5 ch. followed by Qg7. So g6 is forced, and now White wins the exchange by Bxf8.

5

THE OPENINGS

Introduction

It has been seen that a game is divided arbitrarily into three phases, the opening, the middle game and the end game. An advantage gained in the opening will be carried into the middle game; so it follows that the opening will tend to shape the course of a game.

Chess openings have, as might be expected, provided the chief source of research for analysts down the ages. Fortunately no perfect opening has been discovered: the subtleties of a game invented by man transcend man's breadth of knowledge – and seem likely to do so for ever.

Nevertheless, chess scholars have succeeded in determining and classifying the best of the initial moves for both sides to various degrees of profundity. The net result of these years of constant research proves only that there is no proof; that if both players adopt the best lines of play, the game will remain approximately level. Theory is always changing – there are schools of thought in chess as in literature – and what was considered best a hundred years ago is classed as only mediocre today. Since analysis is recorded and published, however, the sum of our knowledge of the openings is constantly increasing – not a month passes without new discoveries, of greater or lesser importance, being added to this sum. Even a quite elementary book on the openings will bewilder the new player, conveying the impression that chess is a profound esoteric science rather than a game. Page upon page of continuations, prefaced by exotic names and punctuated with seemingly endless footnotes, each subdividing into further enumerated variations, are enough to frighten the most composed and self-confident of novitiates.

Such works, however, are rarely treated as more than sources of reference; mentors to indicate the pitfalls that attend the unwary, surgeons to assist the student conducting his own post-mortem.

A good player will follow a book line without being conscious of doing so – simply because his moves are the best in the position with which he is confronted and, in consequence, are listed in the opening compendiums.

The purely "book" player, moving "according to Hoyle", will be at a disadvantage if the opponent deviates from the accepted line. In order to play chess openings well, it is not only essential that an elementary knowledge of the approved lines is acquired, but, more important, that the ideas that activate these lines are clearly understood.

Openings are loosely divided into "open" and "close" games.

Open games are those in which the pieces are developed quickly, and the play is directed chiefly along tactical lines – games commencing: 1. e4, e5 are mostly in this category; close games are those in which play develops along strategical lines (for example: 1. d4, d5). Broadly speaking, pieces are posted *in front* of the pawns in open games, *behind* the pawns in close games. Certain openings fall between these two groups and are classed as "half-open".

There are about a score of important openings and several hundred minor and branch openings recognized. In each of these there are variations and sub-variations.

Some of these openings are acknowledged as better than others, but in general choice of opening is dependent upon style; players selecting lines of play (so far as it is in their power to do so) most suited to their temperament.

The majority of openings commence with: 1. e4 or d4. Occasionally one of the bishops' pawns is advanced, or a knight brought out first, but never a wing pawn. Openings that begin: 1. d4 – the close and half-open games – usually have deep-rooted ideas and involve long-term strategy, and are therefore best avoided in the early stages of a player's development. In this chapter attention will be mainly directed to those openings arising from: 1. e4.

All opening theory is based on the control of the centre, the importance of which has already been demonstrated. Control may be effected in three ways:

(1) Occupation – by the establishment of pawns and/or pieces on the centre squares.

(2) Delayed occupation – by permitting the opponent to occupy the centre at first, then attempting to undermine and break up the position.

(3) Remote control – by commanding the centre from a distance by means of the pieces without actually occupying the squares. In this technique one or both bishops are fianchettoed.

Gambits

It is quite common in the opening to sacrifice a pawn (or even occasionally a piece) in order to gain time in development. An opening sacrifice of this nature is called a gambit. There are a number of recognized gambits, the most common being the King's Gambit and the Queen's Gambit, in both of which a pawn is offered.

Amongst strong players, an extra pawn on one side in the opening, provided other factors – time and space, that together govern position – are equal, is sufficient to win.

With average club players of experience, a minor piece ahead will usually prove decisive. From this it will be seen that a strong player who succeeds in refuting a gambit and obtaining equality in position is well on the way to victory.

An Opening (1)

After this superficial survey of opening theory, let us follow an established method of opening, endeavouring to understand the principles underlying the play. The reader may pass straight on to the next chapter, returning to the study of the openings after mastering middle and end game play.

White	*Black*
1. e4	**e5**

Black could also reply here 1. . . . c5 (the Sicilian Defence); 1. . . . e6 (the French Defence); 1. . . . c6 (the Caro-Kann Defence); 1. . . . Nf6 (Alekhine's Defence); 1. . . . d5 (the Centre Counter) etc. This will give an idea of the choice open to the second player at the start of a game. Each of these defences has its own characteristics and its own advocates. After White's initial pawn advance, Black is in a position to dictate, to a great extent, the future course of the game.

2. Nf3	**Nc6**

We have already seen that both of these are good moves.

3. Bc4	Bc5

These three moves give the opening its name – the Giuoco Piano. The Giuoco is characterised by the quick development of the pieces and direct play in the centre. These straightforward aims recommend it to the student.

4. c3

Preparing the advance of the d-pawn.

4. . . .   **Nf6**

4. . . . d6 is a good alternative. Black's move attacks the undefended e-pawn. To attempt to delay the advance of White's d-pawn by 4. . . . Qf6 would be bad as it violates opening principles: (1) it takes away the best square for the king's knight. (2) The queen is vulnerable to attack here. White might then continue 5. d3 (threatening 6. Bg5, driving the queen to a bad square) and after 5. . . . h6; 6. Be3, d6; 7. Nbd2 Black would be far behind in development.

5. d4   **exd4**
6. cxd4

The black bishop is again attacked, and since the queen's pawn is twice protected, capture would only result in the loss of a piece. The white pawn on d4 is referred to as the d-pawn or the queen's pawn, even though it started life on c2. Pawns, unlike pieces, assume the name of the file on which they stand.

6. . . .   **Bb4 ch.**

A check to some purpose, as will be seen. No check should be made just for the pleasure of announcing it.

7. Bd2	Bxd2 ch.
8. Nbxd2	

Both white knights can capture the bishop, but this move develops another man. Also, if 8. Nfxd2, Nxd4 and Black has won a pawn. If 8. Qxd2, Black replies Nxe4, again winning a pawn. 8. Kxd2 would be bad: (1) it would permit Black 8. . . . Nxe4 ch.; (2) White would thereby surrender the privilege of castling; (3) the move would not develop a man for attack.

8. . . .	d5!

Black strikes at the right moment.

9. exd5	Nxd5

If now 10. Bxd5, Qxd5; White would be saddled with an isolated centre pawn, difficult to maintain since it cannot be supported by another white pawn.

10. Qb3

Attacking the king's knight twice.

10. . . .	Nce7

Not 10. . . . KN moves; 11. Bxf7 ch. nor 10. . . . Be6; 11. Qxb7.

11. 0–0	0–0

Both sides castle king's-side and the position in diagram 39 is now reached. Black has equalised.

DIAGRAM 39

POSITION AFTER BLACK'S 11TH MOVE

Opening (2)

Another example of the Giuoco Piano, in which White gains the ascendency.

	White	Black
1.	e4	e5
2.	Nf3	Nc6
3.	Bc4	Bc5
4.	c3	Nf6
5.	d4	exd4
6.	cxd4	Bb4 ch.

So far, the same as the previous example.

7. Nc3

White, instead of interposing the bishop (the more passive line), sacrifices a pawn for speedy development.

7. . . .   **Nxe4**
8. 0–0

White is now threatening Nxe4. Note that before castling there was no threat as the QN was pinned by the bishop.

8. . . .   **Bxc3**
9. d5!

DIAGRAM 40

POSITION AFTER WHITE'S 9TH MOVE

A surprising move. Instead of recapturing the bishop,

White attacks another piece. Black has now two pieces attacked simultaneously by pawns, an undefended knight in a precarious position and a king in considerable danger. To compensate, Black is a piece and a pawn ahead.

9. . . .	Ba5
10. dxc6	

White regains the piece and is now only a pawn in arrears.

| 10. . . . | 0–0? |

Black castles at the wrong moment. Correct was 10. . . . bxc6.

11. Qd5

A good example of when a queen may be brought out with safety in the opening. Black has two undefended men: the bishop on a5 and the knight. The queen now attacks them both.

| 11. . . . | Nd6 |

The only move. Black prepares a counter. If now 12. Qxa5, Nxc4.

12. Bd3

White now threatens to win a piece with Qxa5.

12. . . .	Bb6
13. Bxh7 ch.	

And here we are at the typical B/Q/N attack on the castled king (diagram 16). Black can only avoid mate by ruinous loss of material. A good sample of an open game: highly tactical, with time as valuable a commodity as force. In a close position, a player may make four or five consecutive moves with a knight in order to post it on a good square, whereas even two such moves in a game like this could result in calamity.

Opening (3)

White	Black
1. e4	e5
2. Nf3	Nc6
3. Nc3	Nf6

Now all four knights are in play and the position is solid on both sides. This opening is known as the Four Knights' Game, and since it is lacking in punch – White's third move could hardly be called aggressive – it is favoured, in general, by those who like to "play safe".

4. Bb5	Bb4
5. 0–0	0–0

The development of both sides has been logical. First the knights came out, then the freed bishops before the d-pawns are advanced to free the remaining bishops. Both sides then castled so that after the advance of the d-pawns, the queens' knights would not be pinned.

6. d3	d6
7. Bg5	

Pinning the knight. White is threatening the powerful Nd5 putting further pressure on the pinned piece.

7.	. . .	Bxc3
8.	bxc3	h6

Attacking the bishop. Black cannot afford to release the knight by moving the queen, since White would then exchange bishop for knight when Black, being compelled to recapture with the g-pawn, would be left with a weak king's position. Often in the opening a knight can be unpinned by Qd6, a move which allows the recapture with the queen should the knight be taken. This move is not, of course, possible here as d6 is occupied by a pawn.

9. Bh4		Qe7

Black dare not now play g5 to release the knight, as the king's position would then become very weak. White could sacrifice with advantage: 10. Nxg5, hxg5; 11. Bxg5, and the knight remains pinned with the black king deprived of all pawn shelter. Since Black did not intend to follow up the attack on the bishop, what was the point of h6? This type of position occurs in almost every opening and its anatomy is worth attention. The move does not lose time since the bishop is compelled to retire, and its importance lies in the fact that g5, although not immediately practical, can be held in reserve as an option should the need arise. Further, the move provides a square for the king at h7 which might prove useful later if back-rank mates threaten (see diagram 18).

10. Qd2

A multi-purpose move. Its merits are worthy of

analysis: (a) it prevents, at least for the time being, g5 since this would be swiftly punished: 10. . . . g5?; 11. Nxg5, hxg5; 12. Qxg5 ch., Kh7; 13. Qxf6 and White stands two pawns to the good. (b) It neutralises the counter-pin 10. . . . Bg4 (c) It unites the two white rooks, which we know to be desirable. (d) It affords protection to the undefended white pawn at c3.

The position in diagram 41 has now been reached. An assessment of the game at this point shows that White stands very marginally better: (a) the pin is still in place; (b) the b-file is open for the white rooks to occupy; (c) White has attack possibilities with an eventual advance of either the d- or f- pawn; (d) White has the slight advantage of the two bishops. Black is solid but has no visible attacking prospects at this stage.

DIAGRAM 41

POSITION AFTER WHITE'S 10TH MOVE

Opening (4)

The King's Gambit was very popular a century ago, less so at the present day. The opening provides a good example of speedy development of the pieces; play is often wild with both sides in peril of a sudden collapse. Here is a typical skirmish:

White	Black
1. e4	e5
2. f4	

This move establishes the opening. Black may now either accept or decline the gambit pawn.

2. ...	exf4

Black can decline the gambit by 2. . . . d5 or 2. . . . Bc5.

3. Nf3

Attacking the centre and preventing 3. . . . Qh4 ch. This early knight move is common to almost all openings and is very rarely inferior.

3. . . .	g5

Black supports the pawn at f4. Notice that the g-pawn is guarded by the queen so White cannot play 4. Nxg5. The yolk of White's game in the King's Gambit is the attack against the weak point in Black's defence: the f7 square. The surrender of the f-pawn by White opens the file for the rook (after castling) to bear indirectly against this weak point. In order to keep the f-file closed, Black endeavours to maintain the advanced pawn, but 3. . . . d6 is less hazardous.

4. h4

Hitting at the support.

4. . . .   **g4**

Black has little option but to advance. If 4. . . . gxh4; Black's pawns are hopelessly weakened and neither f6 nor h6 are playable: (a) 4. . . . f6; 5. Nxg5, fxg5; 6. Qh5 ch., Ke7; 7. Qxg5 ch., Nf6; 8. e5 and White recovers the piece with a winning attack. Or (b) 4. . . . h6; 5. hxg5, hxg5; 6. Rxh8 and wins.

5. Ng5

This variation is known as the Allgaier Gambit.

5. . . .   **h6**

The knight is trapped.

6. Nxf7

White has sacrificed a piece to disrupt Black's king's side.

6. . . .   **Kxf7**

Black has no choice as the rook and queen are forked.

7. d4

Now the bishop attacks the pawn f4. Observe that White concentrates on speedy development. If 7. Qxg4, Nf6; and Black gains time by attacking the queen. 7. Bc4 ch. is also good.

7. . . .   d5

Black must counter-attack quickly but 8. . . . f3 may have been better.

8. Bxf4   Nf6

8. . . . dxe4; allows 10. Bc4 ch., developing another piece. Black is aiming to keep the position as closed as possible. If the Black forces can be marshalled in time, the extra piece will prove a telling advantage.

9. Nc3

Black was threatening 10. . . . Nxe4.

9. . . .   Bb4
10. Be2

White is staking everything on attack. The position now reached is typical of the opening; there are good chances for both sides in practical play, when there is the time factor to be considered (in fact, theoretically lost positions are often won in practice: time is on the side of the attacker). Notice that Black's queen's side is still undeveloped. (See diagram 42 opposite.)

Opening (5)

One of the oldest and most popular openings is the Ruy Lopez, named after a Spanish dignitary of the 16th

DIAGRAM 42

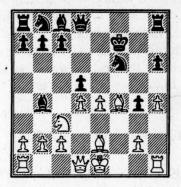

POSITION AFTER WHITE'S 10TH MOVE

Century. Recent analysis shows that the Lopez does not confer the marked advantage to White it was once thought it did, but no one will assert that the last word has been said on this remarkable opening.

The centre remains the focus of action for both sides, but strategy rather than tactics forms the basis of action.

	White	Black
1.	e4	e5
2.	Nf3	Nc6
3.	Bb5	

The purpose of this move is not at once apparent. It does not pin the black knight and the continuation 4. Bxc6, dxc6; 5. Nxe5 is not a threat because of 5.... Qd4! attacking both the knight and the e-pawn, with a good game for Black.

3. . . .   **a6**

Black attacks the bishop immediately with essentially the same idea we saw in Opening (3). Black has several playable moves in this position: 3. . . . Nd4; 3. . . . Nf6; and 3. . . . d6 are examples. The text (i.e., the move played) is probably the best, however, as after the retreat of the bishop Black may still adopt any of these continuations.

4. Ba4   **Nf6**

Black develops a piece, attacking White's e-pawn in the process.

5. 0–0

White ignores the attack, sacrificing the pawn for speed of development.

5. . . .   **Nxe4**

Black had the choice here of two contrasting lines of play. The text opens the game, promising lively play by both sides. The passive 5. . . . Be7 would have been more solid, but would not have presented White with problems. A good example of where players of different temperament and style would diverge.

6. d4

Vigorous play is called for.

6. . . .   **b5**
7. Bb3   **d5**

Black counters in the centre and gives back the pawn. The player who accepts a sacrifice can often return the material at the right moment with advantage. The value of Black's 3rd move is now clear. If it had not been played, White would have exchanged the bishop for the knight at the right time, hindering or even preventing the advance of Black's d-pawn.

8. dxe5

Nxe5 was also playable.

8. ...   **Be6**

White was threatening to capture the d-pawn.

9. c3

Securing the square d4 and allowing the king's bishop to be brought into play on the king's side.

9. ...   **Be7**

Bc4 would be bad as then the Ne4 would have had no escape square for White's e-pawn is attacking both d6 and f6.

10. Nbd2   **0-0**
11. Qe2

Threatening to win a pawn by 12. Nxe4, dxe4; 13. Qxe4.

11. ...   **Nc5**

An inexperienced player might prefer 11. . . . Nxd2. The move would be weak however, because it would exchange off a piece that has no immediate use and it would bring White's bishop into play thereby uniting the rooks.

12. Nd4

This move accomplishes several things. It stops the advance of the d-pawn, attacks Black's knight, and allows the f-pawn to advance with consequent gain in mobility for the rook behind it. The queen's knight now has a good square to move to, releasing the bishop. It is pleasing to see how positions unfold in this manner, each man gracefully moving into its place in the opening framework.

This would be a good point to leave the game, which is on the point of entering the middle game stage. White is playing for a K-side attack, with the aim of keeping the centre and the queen's wing closed. Black, on the other hand, has no chances on the K-side, and will play for a Q-side attack. Note that Black has the pawn majority on the queen's wing. White on the king's wing, and alignment which is conducive to a two-wing struggle. In the position, Black's immediate aim is to play c5 as soon as possible – an objective which will be resisted by White. So long as the c-pawn remains backward, Black will be unable to assert superiority on this side. Broadly speaking, White may be said to have kept the advantage of the initial move.

Opening (6)

In the 1890's a great American authority wrote that the Queen's Gambit "is now rarely met with in serious play." If he had lived another thirty years he would have seen the

DIAGRAM 43

POSITION AFTER WHITE'S 12TH MOVE

opening established as one most favoured in master tournaments.

Compared with the King's Gambit, the Queen's Gambit is dull in the sense that there is little action in the initial stages. Both sides concentrate on developing their forces, which is accomplished without undue interference.

White	Black
1. d4	d5
2. c4	

The Queen's Gambit. As in the King's Gambit, Black may now accept or decline the proffered pawn, but whereas in the King's Gambit acceptance of the pawn is normal, the reverse is true of the Queen's Gambit.

2. . . .   **e6**

This move shuts in the QB, the development of which is the chief headache for Black in this opening. Black can obviate the problem by playing here 2. . . . c6 (the Slav Defence), keeping the diagonal clear for the bishop, but it also has its disadvantages. If the Black d-pawn is left unattended, White gains time and a powerful centre with 3. cxd5, Qxd5; 4. Nc3 followed by 5. e4.

3. Nc3   **Nf6**

White covets control of the two white squares in the centre. Black's move counters the attack.

4. Bg5

Pinning the knight, thereby neutralizing its restraining influence on the centre.

4. . . .   **Nbd7**

Setting a trap whilst developing a piece. If White now continues 5. cxd5, exd5; 6. Nxd5?, Nxd5!; 7. Bxd8, Bb4 ch.; 8. Qd2 (White has no option), Bxd2 ch.; 9. Kxd2, Kxd8 and Black has won a piece.

5. e3   **Be7**

White frees the king's bishop and also threatens cxd5 as now the king would have an escape square (e2) after the bishop check. Black's reply unpins the knight, and if now: 6. Bxf6, Nxf6 and not Bxf6, losing a pawn after 7. cxd5, exd5; 8. Nxd5.

6. Nf3

A quiet developing move asserting White's control of e5.

6. . . .   **0-0**
7. Rc1

The order of moves is important. The position is pregnant with possibilities, and as so often in chess, the most interesting variations are those which are not played.

7. . . .   **c6**
8. Bd3   **dxc4**

Black waits until after the bishop has moved before capturing the pawn, thereby causing White to lose time.

9. Bxc4   **Nd5**

Black, whose pieces need air, must find a good square for the queen's bishop.

10. Bxe7   **Qxe7**
11. 0–0   **Nxc3**
12. Rxc3   **e5**

Black has at last succeeded in playing e4, freeing the bishop, but White is ahead in development.

13. dxe5

White decides to dissolve the centre.

13. . . .   **Nxe5**

14.	Nxe5	Qxe5
15.	f4	

We now reach a position (diagram 44) commonly arrived at in the Queen's Gambit. Although White has more pieces in play, Black's position is solid, and with correct play a draw should result.

DIAGRAM 44

POSITION AFTER WHITE'S 15TH MOVE

Opening (7)

We have seen that Black has several good defences to 1. e4 without replying 1. . . . e5; so too in answer to 1. d4, Black is not obliged to respond 1. . . . d5 immediately. Popular is 1. . . . Nf6, which may lead into several defences. Here is the King's Indian Defence in which Black does not immediately challenge in the centre.

White	Black
1. d4	Nf6
2. c4	g6
3. Nc3	Bg7

White prepares to take charge of the centre whilst the black bishop positions itself on the long diagonal.

4. e4	d6
5. f4	

The Four Pawns' Attack. This mass advance looks formidable but conversely it presents Black with a target. The advanced pawns are often difficult to defend and are thereby forced into further advances. 5. Be2 is a more circumspect line for White.

5. . . .	0-0
6. Be2	c5!

Striking at White's d-pawn. If 7. dxc5, Qa5; threatening Nxe4 and Black's development is excellent.

7. d5	e6

A further undermining of the advance. If 8. dxe6, Bxe6; followed by Nc6. Black has a backward d-pawn but plenty of freedom.

8. Nf3	exd5
9. cxd5	

Also playable is 9. exd5 when White relinquishes all idea of advancing the centre pawns.

9. . . .   **b5**

Threatening 10. . . . b4 followed by Nxe4 when the white knight moves, yet apparently losing a pawn for nothing. But after 10. Bxb5, Nxe4; 11. Nxe4, Qa5 ch.; 12. Kf2, Qxb5; 13. Nxd6, Qa6; 14. Nxc8, Rxc8; Black has a good game and value for the pawn lost with the white king dangerously exposed (diagram 45).

DIAGRAM 45

POSITION AFTER BLACK'S 9TH MOVE

Opening (8)

In opening (1), several other defences to White's initial e4, other than e5, were mentioned. One of these, the Sicilian, is a very popular choice for the fighting player; it meets thrust with thrust and counter-thrust with counter-thrust.

	White	*Black*
1.	**e4**	**c5**

Threatening to take off the d-pawn should it advance.

2.	Nf3	d6
3.	d4	cxd4
4.	Nxd4	Nf6
5.	Nc3	g6

Black prepares to fianchetto the king's bishop – the Dragon variation.

6.	Be2	Bg7
7.	Be3	Nc6
8.	0–0	0-0
9.	Nb3	Be6

Both sides are now preparing to attack, White on the king's side (notice the two bishops and the f-pawn poised for assault) and Black on the queen's side (Black's king's bishop, although screened, is trained on White's rook at a1).

10.	f4

Attack!

10.	. . .	Na5

Counter-attack!

11.	f5	Bc4
12.	Nxa5	Bxe2

Not of course 12. . . . Qxa5; 13. Bxc4.

13.	Qxe2	Qxa5
14.	g4	

White flings caution to the winds. Should the attack fail and the majority of the pieces stay on the board, White's king will be difficult to defend.

> **14. ...**   Nd7
> **15. Nd5**

So far, White has had most of the game and has a slight advantage in position, but Black has plenty of fight and if White pauses a reversal of fortunes is likely. It is on this razor-blade margin between success and failure that the appeal of the opening rests.

DIAGRAM 46

POSITION AFTER WHITE'S 15TH MOVE

Opening (9)

The French Defence is an ideal opening for the patient

player. Black allows White to build up a strong pawn centre and then harasses it from van to rear. As in the Queen's Gambit, Black's chief worry is the development of the queen's bishop which is imprisoned by the very first move.

White	Black
1. e4	e6

It is this move that gives the opening its name.

2. d4	d5

The almost invariable second moves.

3. e5

This advance is often delayed.

3. . . .	c5

Hitting immediately at the support of the e-pawn.

4. c3	Nc6

Keeping up the pressure on White's d-pawn.

5. Nf3	Qb6
6. Be2	cxd4
7. cxd4	Nge7
8. b3	

The queen's bishop must be developed.

8. . . .	Nf5

Black brings the second knight to bear on the d-pawn which has now been deprived of its pawn support.

    9. Bb2   **Bb4 ch.**
   10. Kf1

DIAGRAM 47

POSITION AFTER WHITE'S 10TH MOVE

The only move, for if a piece is interposed the d-pawn falls. An assessment of the position (diagram 47) reveals that White has so far maintained the pawn at e5, a powerful wedge in the centre. Black however still has three pieces trained on the weak d-pawn and has prevented White from castling whilst retaining a solid defence position. A factor in favour of White, and by no means obvious, is the mutual interference of the black bishop at b4 and the knight at f5. Both can be attacked by pawns and both would then best be placed at e7. White will now bring the king to g2 after advancing the g-pawn and may attack with almost equal facility on either side. Black will rely for defence on a sound position and the pressure on the d-pawn. Note that Black's game is cramped and that the bishop at c8 is still undeveloped – two typical features of the French.

Summary

The examples given above are not arranged in any kind of order but they are generally representative of their respective openings and run the gamut from the patently aggressive (King's Gambit) to the stolidly defensive (French Defence).

But how, the reader asks, am I to assimilate a seemingly endless string of variations, where the first slip may prove dangerous if not fatal?

Fortunately there is no need to learn more than one or two openings. For example, with the white pieces you will be able to play the English Opening (1. c4) with little fear of your opponent transposing it into another. As Black, in reply to: 1. e4, the French, Sicilian or Caro-Kann are three good resources at your disposal, and you can specialise in one of these. After: 1. d4, the Dutch Defence (1. . . . f5) leaves White little option but to follow the normal course of the opening.

If, on the other hand, you open: 1. e4 yourself, your opponent will be able to choose a pet defence – a factor which will offset the advantage of the move.

However, the adoption of selective lines, based on personal preference of style, should be left until you have acquired a thorough working knowledge of the theory of the game. Until you are reasonably sure of yourself, the advice offered earlier still applies: 1. e4 is the best opening move.

It is said that one cannot ride a horse properly until one has been thrown a few times. The same holds good for chess; more being learned from a few opening debâcles than this, or any other chapter could impart.

Major Openings

A short list of the openings commonly met with is given below in alphabetical order. In each example, try to visualise the central pawn structure, the development of the pieces and the strategical aims of each side. It sometimes happens that one opening transposes into another (for example, a Petroff becomes a Four Knights'). Artful transpositions have become a technique of modern master play.

Albin Counter-Gambit (1. d4, d5; 2. c4, *e5*; followed after 3. dxe5 by 3. . . . d4). Black surrenders a pawn for the sake of quick development. Generally good for White.

Alekhine's Defence (1. e4, *Nf6*). Black entices the white pawns to advance by offering the king's knight as a target. Normally slightly favourable to White.

Benko Gambit (1. d4, Nf6; 2. c4, c5; 3. d5, *b5*). A modern gambit which White generally finds safer to decline.

Benoni (1. d4, *c5*). A relatively recent addition to Black's repertoire, more often seen in the form of the Modern Benoni (1. d4, Nf6; 2. c4, c5).

Bird's Opening (1. *f4*). A doubtful move since it exposes the white king to attack. Not much played.

Bishop's Opening (1. e4, e5; 2. *Bc4*). Can be transposed into several well-known lines.

Caro-Kann Defence (1. e4, *c6*). A popular defence to the king's pawn, the Caro-Kann is sound but unambitious. It avoids the drawback of the French – shutting in of the queen's bishop – but has other problems. Slightly favourable to White.

Centre Counter (1. e4, *d5*). Black immediately counters in the centre. Vigorous play, normally with some advantage to White.

Centre Game (1. e4, e5; 2. *d4*). White relies on the initiative and breaks open the centre at once. Equal chances.

Danish Gambit (1. e4, e5; 2. d4, exd4; 3. *c3*). Followed, after 3. . . . dxc3 by 4. Bc4, cxb2; 5. Bxb2. A projection of the Centre Game, the Danish gives White good chances in practice despite the loss of the two gambit pawns, due to the free development obtained for the pieces.

Dutch Defence (1. d4, *f5*). Black aims at controlling e4. The game is usually close in the early stages. White has slightly the better of it as a rule.

English Opening (1. *c4*). The fianchetto of the king's bishop is normal for the first player. White is often playing the Sicilian Defence with a move in hand but Black has several good lines.

Evans Gambit (1. e4, e5; 2. Nf3, Nc6; 3. Bc4, Bc5; 4. *b4*). The Evans offers White many compensations for the pawn; a strong centre, quick development and good attacking chances. The refutation, as is often the case with gambits, is for Black to give the pawn back at the right moment.

Flank Openings. A whole complex of openings, grouped under this general heading, has enjoyed increased popularity in recent times. As the description suggests, these openings are characterised by the avoidance of an early occupation of the centre, at least by one side. The fianchetto of one or more bishops is a common feature. The aim is a timely central pawn advance. The Flank Openings include the King's Indian Attack, the Pirc, Robatsch and some lines of the English, the Reti and others. A side which avoids early occupation of the centre must play energetically or be overwhelmed, whilst the side which occupies the centre first must be careful to avoid compromising the pawn structure.

Four Knights' Game (1. e4, e5; 2. Nf3, Nc6; 3. Nc3, *Nf6*). A solid opening giving little advantage to the first player.

French Defence (1. e4, *e6*). A common reply to e4. Both players now advance their queens' pawns when Black has a secure but rather restricted position. Popular with positional players who are content to work for an end game advantage. White usually plays for a king's side attack.

Giuoco Piano (1. e4, e5; 2. Nf3, Nc6; 3. Bc4, *Bc5*). A very old opening. Sharp attacks by either side are not uncommon. Equal game.

Grunfeld Defence (1. d4, Nf6; 2. c4, g6; 3. Nc3, *d5*). After the usual 4. Nf3, Bg7 (diagram 48) Black aims to exploit the a1–h8 diagonal on which White is weak.

King's Gambit (1. e4, e5; 2. *f4*). Once one of the most popular openings, the King's Gambit is now rarely played as White's second move is considered too loosening. The gambit is the starting point of many adventurous lines: the Allgaier, Bishop's Gambit, Kieseritzky, and Muzio are examples. The pawn offer may either be declined or accepted. In either case, Black has an easy game with correct play. The opening is highly tactical.

DIAGRAM 48

THE GRUNFELD DEFENCE

King's Indian Defence (1. d4, Nf6; 2. c4, g6; 3. Nc3, *Bg7*). Now one of the most popular defences, giving Black good chances. White usually adopts one of two general systems: a large pawn centre with the king's bishop posted at e2 or d3, or a less ambitious pawn advance with the bishop posted at g2. Black sometimes has difficulty in finding good squares for the minor pieces. The King's Indian can easily transpose into one or other of the Flank Openings.

Nimzo-Indian Defence (1.d4, Nf6; 2. c4, e6; 3. Nc3, *Bb4*). A popular and versatile defence, described as the equivalent of the Ruy Lopez in the Queen's Pawn Game (q.v.). A game of strategic possibilities.

Nimzo-Larsen Attack (1. *b3*). As with most Flank Openings, White plans to control the centre by indirect play. Black should have no difficulty in equalizing.

Petroff's Defence (1. e4, e5; 2. Nf3, *Nf6*). Black counterattacks at once. A sound reply to 1.e4, usually good for a draw with best play.

Philidor's Defence (1. e4, e5; Nf3, *d6*). White gets the more mobile game as Black's king's bishop is shut in.

Pirc (1. e4, d6; 2. d4, *Nf6*). A resilient but rather passive defence.

Queen's Gambit (1. d4, d5; 2. *c4*). Like the King's Gambit, the starting point of several opening systems; for example, the Queen's Gambit Accepted (not often seen), the Tarrasch, the Catalan, the Cambridge Springs. Popular until recent years when the King's Indian and Flank Openings came into favour on account of their greater flexibility.

Queen's Indian Defence (1. d4, Nf6; 2. c4, e6; 3. Nc3, b6; 4. g3, *Bb7*). Black aims to control e4 and prevent the advance of White's e-pawn. White prepares to face bishops on the diagonal.

Queen's Pawn Game (1. d4, *d5*). White plans a more

cautious approach than the Queen's Gambit. Here 2. Nf3 is common.

Reti Opening (1. *Nf3*). Coupled with c4, g3 and Bg2, the aim is control of the centre without occupation in the hope that Black will set up a rigid pawn structure that will then be vulnerable to attack. A typical Flank Opening (q.v.).

Ruy Lopez (1. e4, e5; 2. Nf3, Nc6; 3. *Bb5*). One of the oldest and most popular of openings, the Ruy abounds in complex strategical ideas in which the strongest player is likely to come out on top.

Scotch (1. e4, e5; 2. Nf3, Nc6; 3. *d4*). After 3. . . . exd4; 4. Nxd4, the Scotch Game, there are few terrors for the second player. White can instead give up the pawn with 4. Bc4, the Scotch Gambit, but Black should have no difficulty in withstanding the attack.

Sicilian Defence (1. e4, *c5*). Nowadays the most popular defence to 1. e4. Generally, White plays an early d4 when Black exchanges pawns and attempts to play d5 when it is safe to do so. Debâcles in this opening are not uncommon but results are evenly balanced.

Slav Defence (1. d4, d5; 2. c4, *c6*), also the Semi-Slav (1. d4, d5; 2. c4, c6; 3. Nc3, *e6*). A resourceful and interesting defence to the Queen's Gambit. The Meran System (which either side can avoid) is an exciting variant of the Semi-Slav offering equal chances.

Two Knights' Defence (1. e4, e5; 2. Nf3, Nc6; 3. Bc4, *Nf6*). An alternative to the Giuoco Piano 3. . . . Bc5. Interesting play follows 4. Ng5 attacking the weak f-pawn. On the whole, chances are about even.

Vienna (1. e4, e5; 2. *Nc3*). Gives a fairly equal game. After 2. . . . Nc6; 3. f4, we have the Vienna Gambit, not dissimilar to the King's Gambit.

6

THE MIDDLE GAME

Introduction

In the opening and the end game the chessplayer can fall back to a considerable extent on the labour of others.

In the middle game, however, you are on your own.

Very little clear-cut instruction can be given on this phase of the game, but there exists an extensive field of theory. A lot of this theory is based on personal preferences, but certain aims, and the means of achieving these aims, are endorsed by all authorities. It is with this field of accepted theory that we are concerned in this chapter.

The Importance of the Centre

A lot has been said already on this subject. Pawns and pieces established on, or controlling, centre squares also exert their influence on both wings.

Pieces, we know, have greater scope when in the middle of the board. A knight posted on a central square can be transferred to any position in two or three moves whereas a knight on the edge of the board would require several moves to reach a vital point on the other wing.

As in warfare, the break-through in the middle is the most effective, the defence forces being split into two camps which, being to a degree interdependent, are the more easily destroyed.

A wing attack, even if successful, may not be decisive. In practice, however, the wing attack is the more common because, as a result of the necessity of central concentration in the early stages of the game, a deadlock is frequent here.

Exchange of Men

The vexed question of when and when not to exchange has been long encumbered by prejudice and a distorted sense of what constitutes sportsmanship.

Be guided only by the position; if you are ahead in material, endeavour to force exchanges and so increase your strength ratio; if behind, avoid exchanges, particularly of queens, or bishops of opposite colours. Do not let favouritism affect your judgment: many otherwise good players admit to preferences for this or that piece and avoid exchanging even when to do so would be to their advantage. Ignore the widespread belief that exchanging queens early on in the game is a breach of fair play.

Ask yourself the following questions when contemplating an exchange:

(a) Am I ahead in material and well placed for the end game?

(b) Which of the two pieces, mine or my opponent's, is the stronger or likely to become the stronger?

(c) Am I losing time by taking his piece off, and would it not be better to let mine be taken first?

Let the answers determine your course of action.

Pawns and Pawn Structures

The importance of the pawn structure is difficult to over-estimate. Pawns can be battering-rams for the attack, bulwarks for the defence; and they can also be grave liabilities in either.

Because of the great influence that pawn formations exert on the middle game, and to a lesser degree on the opening and end game, a comprehensive survey of their diverse functions and their merits and demerits are given. Again, generalization has been necessary, and the relative position of the pieces, material and temporal factors must also be taken into account.

Isolated Pawn

A pawn is isolated if there is no friendly pawn on either of the two adjacent files. Because it cannot receive pawn support an isolated pawn is weak.

Doubled Pawns

Pawns are said to be doubled if there are two of the same colour on a file. Doubled pawns are unable to support each other and are particularly vulnerable to attack. Their value is relatively slight (one pawn is able to block two hostile pawns that are doubled). Doubled, isolated pawns are weaker still. Occasionally pawns may be trebled or even quadrupled on a file.

Passed Pawn

A passed pawn is one which is faced with no hostile pawn either on the same file or on one of the two adjacent files.

A passed pawn is a distinct asset, particularly in the ending, since it will command the attention of an enemy piece to restrain its advance.

Backward Pawn

A backward pawn, as its name implies, is a pawn that has been "left behind" and thereby deprived of its pawn support. It is weak because to all intents and purposes it is isolated.

United Pawns

Pawns standing side by side or supporting one another are said to be united. United pawns are strong.

DIAGRAM 49

Diagram 49 gives examples of the pawn types mentioned. The white pawns on b5 and d2 are isolated. The two black pawns on b6 and b7 are doubled and isolated. They are blocked by the single white pawn.

The white pawn on d2 is a passed pawn, notwithstanding that it has not yet moved and is isolated. Black's pawn at g7 is backward; it cannot advance without being captured by the white pawn at f5. Both the pawn formations on the king's side are composed of united pawns.

Pawn Formations

A pawn formation is a series of united pawns; it may be mobile or static in character.

(a) **Mobile.** The strongest mobile formation is line abreast, provided the pawns have ample piece support.

(b) **Static.** The strongest static pawn formation is one in the form of a wedge with the apex in the centre, or a single diagonal chain directed towards the centre. A chain extending outwards from the centre of the board is weak. Diagram 50 will make this clear. The White pawn structure is strong, that of Black weak. White controls by far the greater space. The structure is static (none of the pawns can move) and the play would therefore be confined to the pieces. Such formations are uncommon; but chains of three pawns, as in the last diagram, occur in almost every game at one stage or another.

DIAGRAM 50

United Pawn Structures

Structures of three united pawns are very common, and every combination, together with general remarks on the intrinsic value of each, is given below. For combinations of four or more pawns, the assessment has only to be extended. Orientations and reflections of a basic structure are not included.

DIAGRAM 51　　　　**DIAGRAM 52**　　　　**DIAGRAM 53**

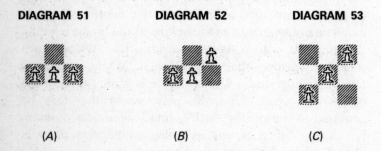

(A)　　　　　　　　(B)　　　　　　　　(C)

(A) Very strong. The pawns command a line of five squares immediately in front of them. If any one is attacked, it may advance one square when it will automatically be defended.

(B) Strong, particularly if the advanced pawn is nearest the centre of the board.

(C) Strong if the apex is towards the centre, weak if away from the centre. Any bishops remaining on the board must also be taken into account. If White has a bishop on the opposite colour to that on which the pawns stand their value is enhanced; on the other hand, if Black has a bishop on the opposite colour it will diminish the value of the structure. The reason for this has already been explained in Chapter 4.

DIAGRAM 54   **DIAGRAM 55**   **DIAGRAM 56**

(*D*)   (*E*)   (*F*)

(*D*) Strong if combined with a bishop on the opposite colour.

(*E*) Moderately strong if the backward pawn is nearest to the edge of the board, weaker if nearest the middle.

(*F*) Generally weak, but if the centre pawn can be advanced will become strong. The "hole" is an ideal post for a hostile piece.

DIAG. 57   **DIAG. 58**   **DIAG. 59**   **DIAG. 60**

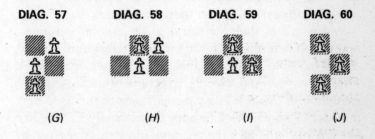

(*G*)   (*H*)   (*I*)   (*J*)

(*G*) Weak, particularly if there is a single black pawn in front of the foremost white pawn.

(*H*) Weak, but slightly better if the double pawn is away from the centre.

(*I*) Weak, but not so weak as (*G*) or (*H*).

(*J*) Very weak. Again the question of the opposite-coloured bishops will arise.

Pawns in Attack

Supposing Black has castled on the king's side, and the moment is propitious for attack. Which pawn or pawns should White advance?

The choice usually falls between the f-pawn and the h-pawn. It must be remembered that pawns are easily blocked by opposing pawns. But a defender will often be compelled to weaken the attacker to make a profitable sacrifice.

White sometimes advances the g-pawn to drive away an enemy piece (usually a knight) at f6, or to attack a pawn that has been played to h6. You must be careful, when advancing like this, not to expose your own king. In this respect the advance of the g-pawn is especially important since it provides the most shelter for the king.

Pawns in Defence

Here we are concerned primarily with the defence of the king after castling, the rules given holding good, however, for defence under most circumstances.

Pawns are at their strongest in their initial positions, and the golden rule is: "Don't move a pawn until you are forced to." The reason for this is that a pawn once moved offers a target and creates structural weaknesses. The exception to this rule is a pawn advance to the third rank in order to fianchetto a bishop. Occasionally a move like f4 by White will block the position, but if this pawn can be attacked by an enemy pawn the measure will only be temporary, and the weaknesses created by the advance may prove to be irreparable.

The defence of the castled king depends to a large extent on the make-up of the attacking forces. Supposing White, who has castled king's side, is under fire from Black. The most vulnerable point is h2 (compared to f2 prior to castling), particularly if Black has retained the king's bishop. White must be careful of the move h3 if

Black's queen's bishop is still on the board, for the sacrifice Bxh3 is a common way to break open the king's position since after gxh3, the king is stripped bare.

The main pawn positions that can arise in front of a castled king, together with remarks on the strong and weak points of each, are given in outline:

DIAGRAM 61   **DIAGRAM 62**   **DIAGRAM 63**

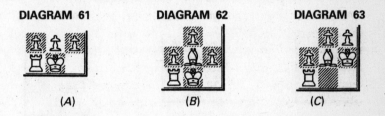

(*A*)   (*B*)   (*C*)

(*A*) Strong; particularly if there is a knight at f3 to guard the h-pawn.

(*B*) Strong; particularly if Black has not the same coloured bishop.

(*C*) Quite strong; but not so favourable as the first two. Vulnerable to pawn attack.

DIAGRAM 64   **DIAGRAM 65**   **DIAGRAM 66**

(*D*)   (*E*)   (*F*)

(*D*) Quite strong if there is also a knight at f3. May be

dangerous if Black has retained the bishop that can attack the h-pawn, or if Black is able to advance the g-pawn with impunity.

(E) Strong; particularly if a knight can be brought to f3.

(F) Weak, but not unduly so, particularly if f4 can be played in safety.

DIAGRAM 67   **DIAGRAM 68**   **DIAGRAM 69**

(G)   (H)   (I)

(G) Very weak if the black queen is on the board supported by one or more of the following: (1) Queen's bishop. (2) One or both knights. (3) A pawn that can be established at f3 or h3 (i.e., either of the holes formed by the advance of the g-pawn). As has been seen in Chapter 4, it is not difficult to mate a king in this position. Of course, if the white king's bishop is still on the board and can be brought to g2 the position immediately becomes strong (see (B)).

(H) Structurally weaker than (G), this pawn formation does not, however, offer Black quite so many mating opportunities, but almost any hostile man established at g3 will prove a source of embarrassment.

(I) Weak. If White has a bishop at g2 and a knight at f3 the position is considerably improved. Black's best way of storming this position is by h5, h4, attacking the g-pawn and threatening by exchange to open the h-file.

General

All other pawn formations in front of a castled king are bad; if the rook has been moved away, each position is proportionately worse. The criterion in all the examples, and in (*G*) and (*H*) in particular, lies in whether Black has adequate force and is sufficiently well placed to carry out an attack. If the end game is reached the pawn structure, so far as the defence of the king is concerned, is inconsequential.

The Pieces

General handling of the pieces in the middle game has already been covered. The bishops and rooks need open lines on which to operate; the knights strong central squares immune from pawn attack. Two bishops co-operate well, covering diagonal side by side. Queen and bishop and queen and knight work together harmoniously as do rook and knight. Two or more pieces exercising the same function on a file, diagonal or rank can be powerful; for example, queen and bishop (the queen in front of the bishop) attacking a square, especially in the field of the enemy king. Also two rooks, rook and queen or two rooks and queen on a file or rank (the queen behind the rook(s) here). As far as the ranks go, the seventh and occasionally the eighth are the only two that come in for consideration, as on these the major pieces are secure from pawn attack.

Strong and Weak Squares

Every move by either side may result in a change of square values. A weak square may be said to be a hole in the pawn formation – the result, in the majority of cases, of a backward pawn. This weak square will be a strong point for the other side, and since, by definition, it is immune from pawn attack, it will be an ideal post for a piece. Weak squares may be only temporarily weak, however. Master-play is entirely concerned with the aggravation and exploitation of weak points.

Open and Close Positions

Blocked positions are not common in chess, although one wing may become paralysed as the result of the rival pawn formations interlocking.

If it is intended to attack on one side of the board it is often advisable to seal the other side in order to forestall any possible counter-attack in that quarter. This can be accomplished by timely pawn advances.

In a close position in particular the ultimate pawn skeleton should be considered with regard to the end game. Such positions afford more opportunity for precise calculation than in open games, as with static or near-static pawn formations the advancing kings will not have to contend with mercurial pawn structures.

In close positions any discrepancy in forces is less marked than in open positions.

In open games, which can arise from close openings it should be noted, the prestige of the pawn suffers; but often exchanges result in some neglected pawn proving the decisive factor.

Piece Traps

There are several traps for winning material that are perennial. It is consequently well worth while to commit them to memory.*

(A) **Knight.** Be careful to leave an escape square for a knight after playing it to the side of the board, otherwise

---

*The examples given are *basic* structures which must be recognised in game settings and are not of course, game positions complete in themselves.

the advance of a hostile pawn may win it. The same care should be taken if a knight is on the fifth rank with an enemy pawn behind controlling the two best escape squares.

Example: (i) WHITE: N on h4, Ps on e5, f2, g2; BLACK: Ps on e6, g7, h7. If White plays 1. f3?, Black wins the knight by 1. . . . g5.

(ii) WHITE: N on e5, Ps on d4, e3, f4; BLACK: K on e8, N on e7, Ps on d5, e4, f7, h5. Black wins the knight by 1. . . . f6.

(*B*) **Bishop.** The trapping of a bishop by pawns was demonstrated in Chapter 4. Another common device is the shutting-in of a bishop that captures an undefended rook's pawn.

Example: WHITE: B on e3; BLACK: R on c8, Ps on a7, b7, c7. If White now takes the pawn – 1. Bxa7, Black plays 1. . . . b6; closing the bishop's escape route and threatening Ra8 and Rxa7.

(*C*) **Rook.** A bishop is sometimes able to shut-in a rook, winning the exchange.

Example: WHITE: R on e4, P on a2; BLACK: B on d6, Ps on a5, b7. If White now attacks the a-pawn, disaster awaits: 1. Ra4?, Bb4 (now the rook cannot escape); 2. a3, b5; winning the exchange for a pawn.

(*D*) **Queen.** A queen can be trapped if she ventures too far into enemy territory, particularly if she has only one line of retreat.

Example: WHITE: Q on a1; BLACK: K on c7, R on d8, B on b7, Ps on a7, b6. If 1. Qxa7?, Ra8 and the queen cannot escape.

The Seventh Rank

In Chapter 4 we remarked on the power of the rook on the seventh rank and we also investigated the potentialities of the discovered check. A type of position not by any means uncommon illustrates the devastating effect of the combination of these two forces: WHITE: R on e7, B on a1; BLACK: K on g8, Q on a8, Ns on d7, f8, Ps on a7, b7, c7, g7. Here the black queen, apparently secure in the corner, falls along with all of Black's queen's side men: 1. Rxg7 ch!, Kh8 (the only square); 2. Rxd7 dis. ch., Kg8; 3. Rg7 ch., Kh8; 4. Rxc7 dis. ch., Kg8; 5. Rg7 ch., Kh8; 6. Rxb7 dis. ch., Kg8; 7. Rg7 ch., Kh8; 8. Rxa7 dis. ch., Kg8; 9. Rxa8.

General Maxims

Before going on to practical examples of middle game play, a few general maxims will not come amiss.

(a) Watch for forks. To someone not familiar with the moves of the men, the fork is a perpetual source of worry, particularly where knights are concerned. Momentary "blindness" also results in casualties from the pawn fork. This accounts, curiously, for a higher relative percentage of victims among more experienced players than the knight fork – possibly because the players are more concerned with strategical considerations and are inclined to overlook the anti-positional move.

(b) Watch the back rank. Even if no immediate danger threatens, a "hole" for the king by moving up a pawn is always a sound investment if time and position permit.

(c) Do not attack undefended pieces for the privilege of driving them to better squares. Such pieces are best left "hanging" as they may become ideal targets for combinations at a later stage.

(d) After castling K-side be careful of advancing the bishop's pawn if the hostile king's bishop can check. There is a prosaic finesse winning the exchange which is common to such positions:

WHITE: K on g1, Q on d1, R on f1, Ps on f4, g2, h2; BLACK: B on e7, N on g4 or e4. White has just played 1. f4?. Play now runs 1. . . . . Bc5 ch.; 2. Kh1, Nf2 ch. (forking king and queen); 3. Rxf2, Bxf2. Black has won a rook for a bishop.

(e) Do not bring rooks into play via the wings. Development of this nature is almost invariably bad.

(f) If you intend to attack be careful to keep a fluid pawn formation: do not block the position or allow your opponent to do so.

(g) Finally, remember that in chess timidity pays no dividends – play aggressively!

Examples from Play: (1) King's Side Attack

When discussing the question of an attack with pawns on a castled king it was pointed out that it is often advisable to castle on the opposite side. Here is a good example of this type of game taken from club play.

	White	Black
1.	e4	e6
2.	d4	d5
3.	exd5	exd5
4.	Bd3	Nf6
5.	Ne2	Be7
6.	Nbc3	c6
7.	Bf4	Bg4
8.	f3	Bh5
9.	Qd2	Nbd7
10.	Ng3	Bg6
11.	Nf5	0-0
12.	Ne2	Re8
13.	g4	

White, having established a strong knight at f5, judges

the moment right for attack. Notice these points:

(a) White's pieces are all in play.

(b) Black's queen's bishop is open to attack from the advancing pawns. Bxf5 would be a mistake, as after gxf5 White would have an open file along which the white rooks would threaten the black king.

(c) White's pawn at f3 immobilises the knight at f6, the square e4 otherwise providing a splendid outpost for this piece.

13. . . .   Nf8
14. 0–0–0   a5

DIAGRAM 70

POSITION AFTER BLACK'S 14TH MOVE

Black correctly appraises that the best chance lies in counter-attack on the queen's wing. However prospects do not look good and the text move is too slow. From now on White dominates the game.

15. h4

White threatens h5, which would force White to take off the knight as the bishop has no escape square.

15. . . .   **h5**
16. Neg3

White wishes to recapture on f5 with a knight, and so sacrifices a pawn to this end.

16. . . .   **hxg4**
17. fxg4   **Nxg4**

These exchanges are fatal for Black, who now opens the g-file as well as allowing the h-pawn to advance.

18. h5   **Bh7**
19. Qe2   **Nf6**
20. Qg2

White has gained time and is in a position to exploit the open file. The immediate threat is the curious 21. Nxg7, and the king would not be able to recapture because of 22. Nf5 dbl. ch., Kh8; and 23. Qg7 mate. The power of the double check is admirably demonstrated: the knight is *en prise* to the bishop and there are notionally three pieces that Black can interpose between the king and the queen. But a double check prescribes a king move and nothing can be done to avert mate.

20. . . .   **Ne6**
21. Be5

Indirectly attacking the weak g-pawn.

21. . . .　　　　　　　Kh8

The black king evades the indirect file attack of the white queen only to walk into the indirect attack of the white bishop on e5. However, there is little to be done.

22. h6　　　　　　　　g6

To avoid the opening of the h-file, which would be terminal, Black is compelled to advance the g-pawn. Now however the N at f6 is pinned and Black cannot escape the loss of a piece.

23. Nxe7　　　　　　　Qxe7
24. Rdf1　　　　　　　Kg8
25. Rxf6　　　　　　　Nf8
26. Nh5　　　　　　　Nd7

Black cannot capture the knight as the pawn is pinned.

27. Bxg6

An example of bulldozer tactics to crush a weak king's position: Black's last defences are stripped.

27. . . .　　　　　　　fxg6
28. Rxg6 ch.　　　　　Bxg6
29. Qxg6 ch.　　　　　Kf8
30. Bg7 ch.　　　　　Kg8
31. h7 mate.

Black watched passively as White's forces gathered strength, instead of initiating early action in the centre or on the queen's side. Black's position was cramped, making it difficult to marshal a defence – notice that at the end of the game, the queen's rook still stood on its starting square.

DIAGRAM 71

FINAL POSITION

One lesson at least may be drawn: it never pays to adopt wait-and-see tactics in the middle game.

Example from Play: (2) The Switch Attack

When engaged in a struggle on one wing, an eye should be kept on the possibility of a quick switch-over to the other wing if the opportunity presents itself.

Here is another game in which White never for one moment loses sight of the whole board.

	White	Black
1.	e4	e5
2.	Nf3	Nc6
3.	Bb5	a6
4.	Ba4	Nf6
5.	0–0	Nxe4
6.	d4	b5
7.	Bb3	d5
8.	dxe5	Be6

Up to here, identical with the game given in Opening (5) in the last chapter.

	White	Black
9.	Qe2	Be7
10.	Rd1	Na5
11.	Nbd2	Nxd2
12.	Bxd2	Nc4
13.	Bxc4	bxc4
14.	b3	cxb3
15.	axb3	

White has gained a positional advantage. The black a-pawn is isolated on a file open to the white rooks. The threat is Rxa6.

	White	Black
15.	. . .	Qc8
16.	Ra5	

This square is momentarily safe from bishop attack so White takes the opportunity of doubling rooks.

	White	Black
16.	. . .	Qb7
17.	Rda1	Bc8
18.	Bg5	

DIAGRAM 72

POSITION AFTER WHITE'S 18TH MOVE

An attempt to prevent Black castling. If Black plays now 18. . . . f6; White wins quickly by 19. exf6 and the black bishop is pinned.

18. . . .	Bb4
19. R5a4	0–0
20. Qd3	Bd7

A trap. If now 21. Rxa6, Bb5!; attacking both rook and queen, would win. However, Black did not expect White to walk the plank; and real intention was to establish the bishop at b5, relieving the weak a-pawn and freeing the queen's rook for action elsewhere. Black is blind to White's plan, although White's last move, coupled with the presence of the two white minor pieces on the king's side were a warning that White might not be wholly concerned with what was happening on the queen's side. The next move comes as a complete shock.

21. c3   Bxa4

Black can do no better than accept the offer of the exchange.

22. Rxa4   Bc5
23. Rh4

Switching to the king's side. White threatens mate on the move by Qxh7.

23. . . .   f5

Black has little option. The other alternatives are worse. (a) 23. . . . g6; permitting Bf6 and a set-up similar to example (h) of Mating Combinations (Chapter 4), when White can force mate in a few moves; or (b) 23. . . . h6; allowing the sacrificial combination 24. Bxh6! and Black's king's position is hopeless. This second type of position – when the king is denuded of pawn protection – has also been referred to previously, an endorsement of how frequently these standard positions can arise.

24. exf6 e. p.

White takes the pawn *en passant*. It cannot be recaptured without quick loss, as Qhx7 ch. is still threatened.

24. . . .   g6
25. Ne5   c6
26. Nxg6

As in the previous game, White sacrifices a piece on g6 to break open the position. Here it cannot be taken without mate in two following (26. . . . hxg6; 27. Qxg6 ch., Qg7; 28. Qxg7 mate).

26. . . .	Rf7
27. Ne5	Re8
28. Qg3	

28. Nxf7 would be a bad mistake. 28. . . . Re1 ch.; 29. Qf1 (forced), Rxf1 ch.; 30. Kxf1, Qxf7 and wins. This bears out the maxim "Watch the back rank".

| 28. . . . | Qa7 |

Black cannot well avoid the double check, for Kf8 or Kh8 would be met with decisive checks from the bishop and knight respectively.

| 29. Bh6 dis. ch. | Kh8 |
| 30. Ng6 ch. | Kg8 |

DIAGRAM 73

FINAL POSITION

Black cannot capture the knight: 30. . . . hxg6; 31. Bf7 db1. ch., Kg8; 32. Rh8 mate.

31.	**Ne7 db1. ch.**	**Kh8**
32.	**Qg7 ch.**	**Rxg7**
33.	**fxg7 mate**	

A delightfully conducted attack. (See diagram 73.)

Examples from Play: (3) The Centre Break-Through

A break-through in the centre in the early stages of the game is not common, since it can only be achieved when the opposition is disproportionately weak. This example shows condign punishment meted out to a timid player.

	White	*Black*
1.	**c4**	**e5**
2.	**Nf3**	**e4**
3.	**Nd4**	**d5**
4.	**e3**	**c5**
5.	**Nb3**	**d4**
6.	**d3**	

White was worried about being left with a backward d-pawn.

6.	**. . .**	**exd3**
7.	**Qxd3**	**Nc6**
8.	**exd4**	**cxd4**

Black has got a passed pawn in the centre. Can it be held? If so, White's game is already bad as the pawn exercises restraint over the white minor pieces. White will

take at least two moves to bring another piece to bear on
the intruder (Nbd2–f3), and meanwhile the queen is
exposed to attack.

9. a3

White is afraid of Nb4 because after 10. Qe4 ch., Be6;
11. Nxd5, Qxd5; 12. Qxd5, Nc2 ch.; 13. K moves, Nxd5;
and Black has won a piece for a pawn. This line is by no
means forced however, and the text is a waste of time.

9.	. . .	Qf6
10.	N1d2	Bf5
11.	Ne4	

This is a mistake, but Black already has command of the
centre.

11.	. . .	Qe6

Pinning the knight and threatening to win it next move.
Observe how the white pieces get tied up in trying to
prevent the loss of this piece.

12.	f3	Nf6
13.	Nd2	

Since the knight on e4 is unable to move, this means the
king's knight.

13.	. . .	0–0–0

Black has succeeded in trussing the defence. The text
brings the rook to guard the advanced pawn. White can do
nothing about the terrible threat of 14. . . . Ne5! attacking the queen and preparing a further advance of the

formidable and now secure pawn.

14. Kd1

To unpin the knight.

14. . . .	Ne5
15. Qb3	d3
16. Nxf6	gxf6
17. Qa4	

Paralysis has set in, and White is reduced to moving the queen again.

17. . . . Bc5

Black guards the a-pawn, brings the last minor piece into play and unites the rooks, all in the one move.

18. Nb3 Nxf3

DIAGRAM 74

POSITION AFTER BLACK'S 18TH MOVE

This sacrifice can hardly be wrong in such an over-whelming position.

19. gxf3

White has no option but to accept: Qe1 mate was threatened. Here 19. Bd2 was useless: 19. . . . Nxd2; 20. Nxd2, Bg4 ch.; 21. Nf3 (not 21. Kc1, Qe1 mate), Rhe8; 22. Kc1 (22. Qa5 is no better), Bxf3; 23. gxf3, Qe1 ch.; 24. Qd1, Be3 ch. etc.

19. . . .   d2

The pawn which has been the cause of all White's troubles is now sacrificed to force the win. Whichever white piece captures (although again there is no option) will be pinned.

20. Bxd2   Rhe8
21. Bh3

White had to prevent mate at e1.

21. . . .	**Qe2 ch.**
22. Kc1	**Bxh3**
23. Re1	**Qxe1 ch.!**
24. Bxe1	**Rxe1 ch.**
25. Kc2	**Bf5 ch.**
26. Kc3	**Re3 mate**

A pleasing finish. Note how White's forces were split in two by the centre thrust and how, until near the end, neither of the white bishops or rooks had even moved. In the final position it will be seen that both the centre files are controlled by the black rooks and both bishops are occupying the best possible squares relative to the position, whereas not one of the white men is well placed.

Examples from Play: (4) The Queen's Side Attack

The Q-side attack differs fundamentally from the K-side attack in that there is no obvious target. This is only true in the broad sense, for in effect any weakness constitutes a target; but a weakness is not strictly a weakness unless it can be exploited. A Q-side attack may be desirable for one or more of several reasons; it may be to counter a K-side attack, it may be because the K-side is either blockaded or barren of opportunity, or it may be because the dispersal of the men is such as to be conducive to action on this wing. In the Q-side attack the balance of pawns engaged is of prime importance. By early exchanges it is common to find one player left with three pawns against two on the Q-side and with, say, three against four in the centre and on the K-side. In any case, the attacker's plan should be governed to a large extent by the pawn ratio and the pawn structure, for weaknesses are created primarily by pawns through their inability to retrace their steps.

The attacker therefore launches an assault with the intention of exploiting (or creating) a weakness in order to achieve an advantage in material, space or time.

The attacker must be prepared to change his plan at any apparent change of weaknesses (i.e., when the defender disposes of one weakness only to create another).

The example appended is from Master play, and I have selected it for its simplicity of idea and execution.

	White	Black
1.	d4	d5
2.	c4	e6
3.	Nc3	Nf6

4.	Bg5	Be7
5.	e3	h6
6.	Bh4	0–0
7.	Rc1	Ne4
8.	Bxe7	Qxe7
9.	cxd5	Nxc3

Not of course 9. . . . exd5; 10. Nxd5!

10.	Rxc3	exd5
11.	Bd3	c6
12.	Ne2	Nd7
13.	0–0	Nf6
14.	Qb1	

Up to here the game has followed well-trodden paths. White now perceives that the king's side is sterile of opportunity, the centre is closed (there is little chance of being able to force e4), and therefore the future of the game lies on the queen's wing.

Although White has the pawn minority on this side (two to three), the Black pieces are not well placed whilst White can manoeuvre freely. The text move prepares the advance of the b-pawn.

14. . . .		a5

Temporarily delaying the advance of the pawn.

15. a3		Bd7

White has succeeded in creating a small weakness in the black position: either the b- or c-pawn is going to be permanently backward.

	16. b4	axb4
	17. axb4	Ra4

Black has obtained compensation in the open rook's file. There follows a typical manoeuvre in which Black moves the rook up to attack an undefended man and is thereby able to double rooks on the file.

18. Rb3

Not 18. b5, cxb5; 19. Bxb5, Rb4; 20. Rb3, Bxb5; 21. Rxb4, Bxe2; 22. Rxb7, Qe4; forcing the exchange of queens and leaving Black with a material advantage. Subtle resources frequently lurk in innocent-looking positions!

	18. . . .	Rfa8
	19. b5	g6
	20. bxc6	Bxc6

Now the black b-pawn is isolated. The d-pawn is also isolated. Black could have avoided both these contingencies by recapturing with the pawn, but then the bishop would have been shut in, a white rook would have been able to occupy the seventh rank, and the advance c5 would probably never have been playable.

	21. Bb5	Ra2
	22. Nc3	R2a3
	23. Rc1	Ng4
	24. Rxa3	Rxa3
	25. Nd1	

Black threatened to give up the knight for a winning

attack by: 25. . . . Nxe3; 26. fxe3, Qxe3 ch.; 27. Kh1, Rxc3.

25. . . .	Qc7
26. g3	

Black threatened Qxh2 ch. White correctly estimates that Black's attack to be of little consequence as Black has not now time to take advantage of White's weakened pawn position.

26. . . .	Qa5
27. Bxc6	bxc6
28. h3	Nf6
29. Rxc6	

The weak pawn falls, and Black has a lost position. Observe how White is now able to turn the flank and to proceed to a direct attack on the black king.

29. . . .	Ra1
30. Qb8 ch.	Kg7
31. Qe5	

Wrong would have been 31. Rxf6, hoping for 31. . . . Kxf6; 32. Qe5 mate because of the reply 31. . . . Rxd1 ch.; 32. Kg2, Qe1; and now White, faced with a mate threat, has nothing better than 33. Rxf7 ch., Kxf7; 34. Qc7 ch., Kf6; 35. Qd6 ch. etc.

31. . . .	Rxd1 ch.

White has not sacrificed a piece because the black knight is pinned and cannot be saved.

DIAGRAM 75

POSITION AFTER WHITE'S 31ST MOVE

32. Kh2   **Qd8**

If 32. . . . Qe1; White gets there first with 33. Qxf6 ch. and mate in two.

33. Rd6   **Qxd6**

There is nothing better. If 33. . . . Qc7; 34. Qxf6 ch., Kh7; 35. Rd8 threatens mate on the move and the queen must be given up. Or 33. . . . Qe8; 34. Qxf6 ch., Kh7; 35. Rd8.

34. Qxd6   **Rd2**
35. Qe5

And Black prolonged the game a few more moves before resigning.

The game, logical throughout, is a lesson in model play on the part of White who created weaknesses and exploited them sufficiently to win a pawn, and then attacked the compromised defence structure that remained. Even if Black had not gone in for the faulty combination that cost the game, it would not have been long before White's extra pawn would have made itself felt. The isolated d-pawn would also have been difficult to defend against the combined assault of the White pieces, and the bolder but swifter death was to be preferred.

Combinations

To give you practice in assessing positions where it is often possible to force immediate wins, some examples from play are given. In all cases White, to move, wins. No solution is longer than six moves, and the examples are given in order of difficulty. Solutions are given at the end.

DIAGRAM 76   DIAGRAM 77

DIAGRAM 78   **DIAGRAM 79**

DIAGRAM 80   **DIAGRAM 81**

Solutions

DIAGRAM 76: 1. Qxh7 ch, Kxh7; 2. hxg6 dbl. ch. and mate.

DIAGRAM 77: 1. Qxh7 ch., Kxh7; 2. Nxf6 dbl. ch., Kh8; 3. Ng6 mate.

DIAGRAM 78: 1. Qxg7 ch., Kxg7; 2. Bc3 ch., Kg6 (Kg8; 3. Nh6 mate); 3. Nf4 mate.

DIAGRAM 79: 1. Bf8 dis. ch., Bh5; 2. Qxh5 ch., gxh5; 3. Rh6 mate.

DIAGRAM 80: 1. Rd8 ch., Rxd8; 2. Qa2 ch. (and now White has the Philidor's Legacy), Kh8; 3. Nf7 ch., Kg8; 4. Nh6 dbl. ch., Kh8; 5. Qg8 ch., Rxg8; 6. Nf7 mate.

DIAGRAM 81: 1. Ra8 ch., Kxa8; 2. Ra1 ch., Kb8; 3. Ra8 ch., Kxa8; 4. Qa1 ch., Kb8; 5. Qa7 ch., Kc8; 6. Qa8 mate.

7

THE END GAME

Introduction

Very few players get excited about the end game; it is the calm after the storm, the anti-climax. This is probably why the average player manages it so badly; certain it is that more won games are dissipated in the ending than in the opening and middle game combined.

There is a tendency to speed up the play when there are only a few men left on the board – and the "obvious" line of play is often the wrong one. The subtleties that exist in this branch of the game are prodigious, and seemingly hopeless positions may be redeemed by witch-like man-oeuvres. There is an old chess adage that runs, "If you see a good move, look for a better one", and nowhere does it hold more true than in the end game.

The first prejudice that must be destroyed is that the end game is stereotyped and uninteresting. It demands imagination, patience and accurate calculation. A study of the various piece and pawn endings also accords a valuable insight into the powers, both latent and active, of the individual chessmen.

The Opposition

In order to begin to understand the theory governing the end game, a clear conception of the "opposition" and what it implies is essential.

If two kings are facing each other on the same file or rank with one vacant square only between them, the player who HAS NOT the move is said to have the "opposition". A corollary is the diagonal opposition – two kings standing on the same diagonal with one vacant square between them. Again the player who HAS NOT the move has the opposition.

The opposition is only considered to be in effect if the player who is not possessed of it has no other man except the king that can be moved without incurring disadvantage.

To have the opposition is almost always desirable, and is often a winning advantage for it permits the king to gain territory at the expense of the enemy king, and perhaps, eventually to penetrate the enemy pawn position.

Look at diagram 82. Here the kings are facing each other and the pawn formations are static and to all intents symmetrical. If Black is to move, White wins. If White is to move the game is a draw.

(a) Black to move. 1. . . . Ke6; 2. Kc5 (the white king is at once able to attack Black's pawns), Ke5; 3. Kxb5, Kd4 (only now is the black king able to pass to attack the white pawns); 4. Kxa4, Ke3; 5. b5, Kxf3; 6. b6, Kxg4; 7. b7, f3; 8. b8(Q) and wins. However, the conclusion requires some care: 8. . . . f2; 9. Qb5, Kf4 (9. . . . Kf3?; 10. Qxg5, f1(Q); 11. Qf5 ch., Ke2; 12. Qxf1 ch., Kxf1; 13. Kb5 and the a-pawn queens); 10. Qe2, Kg3; 11. Kb4, Kg2 (there is nothing better); 12. Qg4 ch., Kh1; 13. Qh5 ch., Kg1; 14. Qxg5 ch., and again White can give up the queen for the f-pawn, marching the a-pawn through to promotion. (There are other ways of winning this ending.)

DIAGRAM 82

Supposing if, instead of 1. . . . Ke6; Black had played 1. . . . Kc6. Now White's task is easier: 2. Ke5, Kc7 (the diagonal opposition, but now tactical considerations take precedence); 3. Kf5, Kd6; 4. Kxg5, Ke5; 5. Kh6 and White promotes the g-pawn quickly. Note that the white king *in advance* and *to one side* of the passed pawn assures its promotion. Black can do nothing; viz: 5. . . . Kf6; 6. g5 ch., Kf7; 7. Kh7 (preventing the black king occupying the promotion square), Kf8; 8. g6, Ke7; 9. g7, Kf7; 10. g8(Q) ch.

(b) White to move. 1. Ke4, Ke6; 2. Kd4, Kd6 and the white king cannot pass, and draw by repetition of moves will follow (see Chapter 1).

Now remove the four pawns on the king's side and study the position again. What result with each player to move? Answer – as before: White to move draws; Black to move, White wins.

(a) Black to move. 1. . . . Kc6 (Black has lost the opposition); 2. Ke5 (White elects to penetrate the fifth rank instead: to have taken the opposition would merely have maintained the status quo), Kc7; 3. Kd5, Kb6 (now the importance of White's Ke5 is evident: Black is obliged again to surrender the opposition in order to protect the undefended b-pawn); 4. Kd6! (White, having gained territory, now takes the opposition), Kb7; 5. Kc5, Ka6; 6. Kc6 (the opposition again: Black is compelled to relinquish the pawn), Ka7; 8. Kxb5, Kb7; 9. Kxa4 and White will have no difficulty in winning.

(b) White to move. 1. Ke4, Ke6; 2. Kd4, Kd6; and we have the same crab-like repetition of moves as before, with neither party yielding ground.

Now replace the four pawns on the king's side and remove the four pawns on the queen's side. Is the result materially affected? The answer is no – White without the move wins, but with the move can only draw.

(a) Black to move. 1. . . . Ke6; 2. Ke4, Kf6; 3. Kd5 (temporarily surrendering the opposition, but penetrating the same rank as the undefended black pawn), Kf7; 4. Ke5 (threatening to win the pawn in two moves), Kg6; 5. Ke6, Kg7; 6. Kf5, Kh6; 7. Kf6, Kh7; 8. Kxg5, Kg7; 9. Kxf4 and wins.

(b) White to move. 1. Ke4, and Black takes up the opposition again by 1. . . . Ke6; forcing a repetition of moves. If Black opts instead to advance among the white pawns the game still ends in a draw: 1. . . . Kc5; 2. Kf5, Kd4; 3. Kxg5, Ke3; 4. Kh5, Kxf3; 5. g5, Ke2; 6. g6, f3; 7. g7, f2; 8. g8 (Q), f1(Q) and since both sides have a king and queen left, the game will be drawn (there are sometimes exceptions to this rule).

The thoughtful reader might ask: Why, in a symmetrical position, does White manage to draw with the move whereas Black loses? Study diagram 82 again. It will be seen that the position is not in fact symmetrical; the white king has the advantage of position. If both kings were moved one rank down the board (to stand on d3 and d5 respectively) the game would be drawn whoever had the move.

King and Pawn v. King

In this ending, the theme is only carried a stage further. Turn back to diagram 11 (Chapter 2). In example (a) White to move wins by Kc6 or Ka6. Because of the pawn at b7 the black king is not able to take up the opposition and must immediately yield ground. This ending (K + P v. K) is simply a fight for the opposition with the odds on the superior force. If a pawn is mobile (not far advanced) it can be used to gain the opposition by interpolating a move.

There are some rules that can be used to guide the player:

(a) With an a- or h-pawn the game is always drawn if the lone king can reach the promotion square or if able to confine the opponent's king on the file in front of the pawn.

(b) If the pawn is advancing level with or in front of the supporting king, the lone king always draws with the opposition.

(c) A king two squares in front of its pawn will always win since a pawn move will ensure the opposition.

(d) A king one square in front of its pawn will win if in possession of the opposition.

King and Pawn v. King and Pawn

The various cases of K and P v. K and P are most important as they are forever recurring. We are not concerned with instances where one pawn immediately falls, or marches through to queen several moves before its rival; but those in which the result may be obscure.

(a) If two pawns stand facing each other away from the edge of the board, and both kings are able to approach the opposing pawns, then the side which approaches first will lose if such approach is not from behind.

WHITE: K on f5, P on d4. BLACK: K on b5, P on d5. 1. Ke5?, Kc4; 2. Ke6 (White is compelled to leave the pawn), Kxd4 and wins. If White approaches from behind, however, the result will be a draw: 1. Ke6, Kc6 (not 1. . . .Kc4?, 2. Ke5 and it is Black who must give up the pawn); 2. Ke5, Kc7; 3. Kxd5, Kd7 and Black has got the opposition.

(b) Where each side has a pawn marching to queen, and the promotions are consecutive, the result is usually a draw, but not always. Here is an exception: WHITE: K on d2, P on h5. BLACK: K on d4, P on a3. 1. h6, a2; 2. h7, a1 (Q); 3. h8(Q) ch., K moves; 4. Qxa1 and wins.

This possibility prompts the necessity for attention to all pre-promotion king moves. WHITE: K on g7, Ps on b2, h6. BLACK: K on c2, Ps on b3, h7. 1. Kxh7, Kxb2; 2. Kg8, Kc3? (this move loses: any other move except Ka1 or Kb1 drew); 3. h7, b2; 4. h8(Q) ch. Now we see the importance of careful king-play. The black king is in check and will not be able to queen the pawn. 4. . . .Kc2; 5. Qh7 ch. (the ending is instructive and is therefore given in full; White must play to drive the black king in front of the pawn by a series of checks, permitting the white king to approach), Kc1; 6. Qc7 ch., Kd1; 7. Qd6 ch., Kc1; 8. Qc5 ch., Kd1; 9. Qd4 ch., Kc1; 10. Qc3 ch., Kb1 (now the white king can approach); 11. Kf7, Ka2; 12. Qc2 (pinning the pawn), Ka1 (not 12. . . . Ka3; 13. Qb1); 13. Qa4 ch., Kb1; 14. Ke6, Kc1; 15. Qc4 ch., Kd1; 16. Qb3 ch., Kc1; 17. Qc3 ch., Kb1; 18. Kd5, Ka2; 19. Qc2 (the same cycle), Ka1; 20. Qa4 ch., Kb1; 21. Kd4, Kc1; 22. Qc4 ch., Kd1; 23. Qd3 ch., Kc1; 24. Kc3, b1(Q); 25. Qd2 mate. If 24. . . . b1(N)ch., Black has insufficient force to draw.

(c) In the foregoing example, Black was left with a king and knight's pawn against king and queen and was unable to save the game. If instead the pawn had been on a bishop's or rook's file the result would have been a draw, due to a stalemate threat.

(i) **Bishop's Pawn.** WHITE: K on g7, P on h7. BLACK: K on d2, P on c3. 1. h8(Q), c2; 2. Qd8 ch., Kc3; 3. Qc7 ch., Kb2; 4. Qb6 ch., Ka1; 5. Qa5 ch., Kb1 (Black always threatens to promote the pawn, giving the white king no time to approach); 6. Qb4 ch., Ka1; 7. Qa3 ch., Kb1; 8. Qb3 ch., Ka1! (instead of moving in front of the pawn, which the king was forced to do in the previous example, the black king moves into the corner for now if White plays 9. Qxc2, Black is stalemated); 9. Qc3 ch., Kb1; 10. Qb3 ch., Ka1 and White can make no headway.

(ii) **Rook's Pawn.** WHITE: K on g7, P on h7. BLACK: K on c2, P on a3. 1. h8(Q), a2; 2. Qh2 ch., Kb1; 3. Qg1 ch., Kb2; 4. Qf2 ch., Kb1; 5. Qe1 ch., Kb2 (not 5. . . . Kc2; 6. Qa1); 6. Qb4 ch., Kc1; 7. Qa3 ch., Kb1; 8. Qb3 ch., Ka1 when Black has no move. To avoid stalemate, White must move the queen away so the white king will never have time to approach.

A lesson to be learned from the above examples is the method of bringing the queen up the board by a series of checks, which can be done vertically, as in (i), or horizontally, as in (ii).

These are the only three cases of K and P v. K and P endings that are likely to cause you any difficulty. There are certain exceptions, but being rare in practical play they are not worth our investigation here. To recapitulate: in the cases where one side queens first, and the other side then advances a pawn to the seventh rank supported by the king on the seventh or eighth ranks (also the sixth rank in the majority of cases), the game is a draw if the pawn is on a bishop's or rook's file, a win for the stronger force if on any other file – always provided, of course, that the other king cannot immediately influence the play. If the second party can only advance the pawn to the sixth rank on the move following promotion, the game is always won by the first party regardless of the position of the kings.

King and Two Pawns v. King and One

This is nearly always a win for the superior force, but there are, nevertheless, numerous positions in which the game is drawn. The two most common cases are:

(i) The two pawns are on opposite wings with the single pawn facing one of them. Suppose White is the superior force in this case. Then White wins by deserting the solitary wing pawn, moving across to the other side of the board, capturing the black man and queening the remaining pawn; for Black must attend to the unwatched pawn, which will march to queen if not intercepted and captured. Only in unusual cases can the weaker force draw in an ending of this nature.

(ii) The three pawns and two kings are more or less together. It is then simply a question again of the stronger party deserting one of the pawns at the right moment and going for the other, or of exchanging a pawn in order to get a won position in the K and P v. K category.

Diagram 83 illustrates four positions not uncommon in this type of ending.

DIAGRAM 83

(a)   (b)

(c)   (d)

(a) Black draws with or without the move. Black has only to keep the king close to the single pawn. If White advances the b-pawn, the resulting exchange will leave White with the a-pawn which, as we know, is insufficient to win.

(b) White wins with an immediate sacrifice regardless of the white king position. 1. g6, hxg6; 2. h7 and queens next move. Or 1. . . . Kf6; 2. gxh7 and the pawn on h6 prevents the black king approaching.

(c) Drawn, regardless of who has the move. White alternates the king between b1 and c2 and any attempt by Black to interfere will result in stalemate.

(d) This position is like (c) but away from the edge of the board. In this and similar positions the stronger force wins, with or without the move. 1. Kg2, Kf4; 2. Kf1, Ke4; 3. Kg2, Kd4; 4. Kf1, Kc3; 5. Kg2, Kd2; 6. Kf1, Kd1; 7. Kg2, Kxe2 and wins.

King and Two Pawns v. King and Two Pawns

This ending, and endings involving more than two pawns a side, are but extensions of those we have already examined. The opposition remains paramount.

A well-known stratagem, not often seen in actual play, is the establishment of a passed pawn when both sides have three pawns, line abreast, facing each other. WHITE: K on h1, Ps on a5, b5, c5. BLACK: K on h3, Ps on a7, b7, c7. Although the black king can reach the pawns first, White wins by : 1. b6, cxb6; 2. a6, bxa6; 3. c6. If 1. . . . axb6; the procedure is the same; viz: 2. c6 etc.

King, Minor Piece, Pawn v. King and Minor Piece

The issue at stake here is a simple one: can the pawn be queened? The important point to remember is that the weaker force has only to sacrifice the piece for the pawn to draw. A simple example will show how important it is for the stronger party to keep the pawn mobile in order to retain any winning chances.

WHITE: K on h1, N on b1. BLACK: K on g3, N on g5, P on e5. 1. Nd2, Kh3?; 2. Nf3 and now 2. . . . Nxf3 gives stalemate, and any other move allows White to capture the pawn leaving Black with insufficient force.

Bishops of opposite colours invariably draw in this type of ending, but with bishops of the same colour the stronger side can often force a victory, the method being to drive the opposing bishop from the vital diagonal by offering an exchange at the moment when such an exchange would yield the opposition. If the opposing king is in front of the pawn, however, and cannot be driven away by checks from the bishop, the game is always drawn.

The N and P v. B and the B and P v. N are the two most interesting – and most common – endings in this category.

In the first case the superior force endeavours to block the bishop diagonal by intervening the knight, and in the second case to force the win by placing the bishop so as to prohibit the knight from approaching the pawn. The power of the bishop over the knight, which is complementary to the knight's power over the bishop, can be seen if a white bishop is placed on e4 and a black knight on h4. Here the knight is unable to move without being captured, although the bishop, in turn, may not move to any of the squares in the knight's field without being exposed to the same risk. This setting is normally unfavourable to the knight, but under certain conditions it may be advantageous, particularly if the bishop is nearer the edge of the board than the knight.

If there are more pawns on the board the matter becomes purely an elaboration of the same theme. The reader is advised to turn back to Chapter 2 for general hints on handling the minor pieces in the ending.

King and Minor Piece v. King and Pawns

With two pawns, this ending is resolved to a case of where the player with the piece will sacrifice it for one pawn in order to be left with the opposition in the ensuing play, thereby assuring the draw.

If the pawns are on opposite sides of the board, or at least separated, the outcome is not difficult to foresee. Two disunited pawns can frequently "squeeze" a bishop: WHITE: K on h2, Ps on b5, g6. BLACK: K on h4, B on e2. White wins by 1. b6, Bf3; 2. g7, Bd5; and now the advance of either pawn will force the bishop to capture, allowing the other to promote. With a knight instead of the bishop the two-pawn "squeeze" is even easier. These cases are, of course, assuming that the kings cannot affect the play.

If a minor piece is opposed by three pawns, it is usually

possible to promote one of the latter with correct play, but there are a number of positions where this ending is only a draw.

Queen and Pawn Endings

In this type of ending the position of the kings is of the utmost importance. If a king is exposed to a series of checks from which there is no sanctuary, the pawn ratio will have no bearing on the game, which will result in a draw.

If, however, the king is able to reach a position of security a mobile extra pawn will be sufficient to win, it being escorted to promotion by the queen.

Rook and Pawn Endings

These are by far the most important, as they are the most common form of ending, due, in part, to the normally retarded development of the rooks in the opening and middle game which enhances their chances of survival.

As has been remarked elsewhere, when both sides have two rooks left the drawing opportunities that present themselves to the side possessed of the inferior pawn position, structurally or numerically, are greater, on average, than occur when each side has only one rook remaining on the board.

The endings involving single rooks and pawns are much the more usual however, and the strategy they embrace may be applied in measure to the positions involving the weightier force.

The main features of this type of ending may be conveniently tabulated.

(a) **Stopping Promotion.** A rook can prevent the promotion of a pawn assisted by a rook by moving onto the same file as the pawn either behind or in front of it. Place a white rook on b8, a black rook on h2 and a black pawn on b2. The black pawn cannot move without being captured, and the black rook is unable to leave the second rank. Note that the white rook can move up and down the file without in any way relaxing vigil on the advanced pawn. Now leave the two black men where they are and place the white rook on b1. Again the black rook cannot leave the rank, but now Black can play Rc2, and the white rook is unable to move along the rank on account of Rc1 followed by b1. From this we see that the rook is best employed *behind* an enemy pawn. In these two examples the black rook is badly placed. Now consider the following position: white rook on b1, black rook on b8 and black pawn on b2. Here it is Black who retains mobility – the white rook is unable to move without allowing the promotion of the pawn. If the white king is able to reach the pawn first it will fall, if the black king reaches it first the white rook will be lost or the pawn will be successfully promoted – the unhappy choice resting with White. If, in the example just given, the two rooks are interchanged, White's position is immeasurably improved for similar reasons.

(b) **The Promotion Check.** This may arise out of the last example, and should be carefully watched. WHITE: K on g2, R on b8. BLACK: K on g7, R on b1, P on b2. The white king is here in the dismal plight of only being able to move backwards and forwards between g2 and h2. Any move to the third rank loses at once: 1. Kg3, Rg1 ch.; and promotes next move. More subtle is the pitfall 1. Kf2?, Rh1!; and if 2. Rxb2, Rh2 ch.; (the "skewer") and the rook is lost.

(c) **Rook and Pawn v. Rook.** The convenient rule for this ending is that if the king of the weaker force can reach the promotion square of the pawn the game is drawn; if it can be prevented from reaching it, the game is won by the stronger force. An exception, as always, is the rook's pawn, which in certain positions is only a draw. There is considerable finesse necessary to consummate the promotion, even after the opposing king has been shut off, as the perpetual check remains a recourse for the weaker player which may not be easily discounted.

(d) **Rook v. Pawn(s).** Two important points to be remembered here. Firstly, that two united pawns that are able to reach the sixth rank without capture will win against a rook, provided that the opposing king cannot interfere: and secondly, that a king and single pawn advanced to the fourth rank or beyond, will draw against a rook provided that the other king is unable to interfere. The first case can be easily proven by just setting the pawns up, placing the rook anywhere on the board where it is unable to capture either of the pawns immediately, and then attempting to arrest promotion. One pawn will certainly fall, but the other will reach the eighth rank safely, and the balance (queen v. rook) is then sufficient to achieve victory.

The second rule is as easy to verify as the first, but why the stipulation "advanced to the fourth rank"? Because, if only on the third rank, the king can be cut off by the rook, the pawn permitted to advance and then attacked and captured before the king can reach it.

Here is an example to clarify the method: WHITE: K on h8, R on a1. BLACK: K on g6, P on h5. With Black to move, the fourth rank is attained by Kg5 and the game is drawn. But White, to play, wins by 1. Ra5, h4; 2. Kg8, h3 (if the pawn is not advanced, the white king will return to decide the issue); 3. Kf8, h2; 4. Ra1, Kg5; 5. Rh1, Kg4; 6. Rxh2 and wins. It will be seen that if the black king had been one square nearer he would have been defending the pawn, and the result would have been a draw.

This "cutting off" of the king is an important feature of rook and pawn end games. An enemy rook ensconced on the seventh (i.e., on the second) rank can be very disturbing if one's king has not left the back rank.

Conclusion

So far we have covered, if very superficially, the entire field of end game play. Many of the points stressed require elaboration and, in certain cases, qualification, but essentially the fundamentals are there. Few average players know more about this phase of the game than these fundamentals, and many are not even conversant with all of them. Three endings from play are now given which demonstrate that charm and subtlety may be concealed in apparently dull positions.

Examples from Play: (1) Pawn Ending

The position in the diagram, with Black to play, was reached in a match-game between two strong amateurs. Pawns are level, and at first glance it appears as though a draw is the likely result. A closer examination will disclose that there is considerably more play in the position than at first meets the eye.

White	*Black*
1. ...	f4
2. e4	

This is forced. If 2. exf4 ch., Kxf4; 3. Kg2, Ke3; and Black will win the f-pawn, and with it the game. To give up the pawn is equally suicidal: 2. Kg2, fxe3; 3. Kf1, Kd4; 4. Ke2, h3; 5. a3, Kc3; 6. Kxe3, Kxb3; winning easily.

Black now observes that White has an uncompromised pawn majority in that theatre of the board bounded by the a- and e-files. Every uncompromised pawn majority (i.e.,

DIAGRAM 84

BLACK TO PLAY

where no pawn is doubled) must yield a passed pawn so any incursion by the black king could prove fatal. For example: 2. . . . Kd4; 3. Kg4, Ke3; 4. b4!, Kd4 (not 4. . . . cxb4?; 5. c5, dxc5; 6. e5 and queens in three moves); 5. bxc5, Kxc5 (5. . . . dxc5; would allow 6. Kf5, when the pawn would march to queen); 6. Kxg5, Kxc4; 7. K x either pawn, winning.

2. . . .	Kf6
3. Kg4	Kg6
4. h3	a5
5. a4	

These pawn moves are important and are often decisive in pawn endings. White has the opposition, and the black king is forced to move, allowing the white king to penetrate. If in the position now reached, White had the move instead of Black, White would have lost, being compelled to advance a pawn: 1. e5, dxe5; 2. b4, cxb4; 3. c5, b3; 4. c6, b2; 5. c7, b1(Q); 6. c8(Q), Qg8 mate.

If instead of 4. . . . a5; Black had played 4. . . . a6; White's reply would have been 5. a3, and not 5. a4?, a5; and Black has the opposition.

5. . . .   **Kh6**

Not of course 5. . . . Kf6; 6. Kh5 followed by Kxg5 winning for White.

6. Kf5

And now it looks as though White is going to force the win.

6. . . .   **Kh5**

White must select from several moves here. The interesting pawn sacrifice: 7. b4 is not quite sound. 7. . . . cxb4 (if axb4; White wins by 8. a5, b3; 9. a6, b2; 10. a7, b1(Q); 11. a8(Q), Qb2 (the only move to stop the threatened mate at h8); 12. Qe8 ch., Kh6; 13. Qg6 mate); 8. c5, dxc5; 9. e5, b3; 10. e6, b2; 11. e7, b1(Q) ch., winning.

The obvious 7. Ke6 is fatal, as White would succumb to the same trap: 7. . . . g4! (Black's uncompromised pawn majority on the king's side is set into motion to yield a passed pawn now that the hostile king is out of range); 8. fxg4 ch. there is nothing better), Kg5; and the f-pawn goes through to queen.

White is therefore left with the alternatives of playing Kf6 or Pe5. If the king advances, the game will be drawn for Black would have nothing better than to return with the king (Kh6) which will result in a repetition of moves.

Black could not now play 7. ... g4; as White could respond 8. hxg4 ch., Kh6; 9. g5 ch., Kh5; 10. g6, h3; 11. g7, h2; 12. g8(Q), h1(Q); 13. Q mates.

Supposing White plays 7. e5, what happens then? Black must capture: 7. ... dxe5 and White can do no better than recapture: 8. Kxe5. Now 8. ... g4 loses for Black. 9. fxg4 ch., Kg5; 10. Ke4, and Black must yield the pawn. After White's 8th move, both sides have a clear majority on one side of the board, and neither can afford to take the initiative in establishing a passed pawn without conceding the game to the other. One illustration will serve to demonstrate this: 8. ... Kg6; 9. b4?, cxb4; 10. Kd4, Kf6; 11. c5, Ke6; 12. Kc4, Kd7; 13. Kd4, and now g4; 14. fxg4, f3; 15. Ke3, b3 wins.

In consequence of these continuations, the game was abandoned as a draw. A highly-instructive end game.

Examples from Play: (2) Bishop and Pawns

This example is also from amateur play. Although pawns are level the bishops are of the same colour – a factor which is important, as we have commented that, in endings of this nature, the side possessing even the slightest advantage in position is often able to force the win.

Here the black king is confined to the edge of the board, and White, with considerable ingenuity, is able to exploit this weakness to secure the win.

White	*Black*
1. . . .	g3

Black has a choice of five plausible moves here, all of which lose. The text appears to be the most promising, for White is unable to play 2. hxg3 on account of 2. . . . h2!

DIAGRAM 85

BLACK TO PLAY

2. Bxa7   **Bf8**

Black cannot play 2. . . . gxh2 as after 3. c5, the mate
4. Bb6 would be unstoppable.

3. Bb8

Threatening 4. Bc7 mate.

3. . . .   **Bc5**

On 3. . . . Kb6; White would have continued 4. a5
ch., Kc5 (b7 is no better); 5. Bxf4 and wins, as after
5. . . . gxh2; 6. Bxh2, Black cannot play Bd6 as this
would permit 7. Bg1 mate.

It is amusing to note that after 3. . . . Kb6; White

would be ill-advised to accept the pawn at once: 4. Bxf4?,
g2; 5. Be3 ch., Bc5; 6. a5 ch., Kxa5; 7. Bxc5, g1(Q);
8. Bxg1 stalemate!

    4. Bc7 ch.   **Bb6**
    5. Bxf4

Threatening Bd2 mate, as the black piece now blocks
the king's flight square.

    5. . . .   **Bc5**
    6. Bc7 ch.   **Bb6**

A vicious see-saw. Compare the example given under
"The Seventh Rank" in the last chapter.

    7. Bxg3

And now White wins comfortably.

Let us examine the other lines available to Black on the
first move:

(A) 1. . . . f3. This loses quickly. 2. c5 (threatening
mate by Be1), Bd2 (the only move); 3. Bh4 and Black
cannot avert the mate at d8.

(B) 1. . . . a6. Now 2. b6! Bf8; 3. c5 (Be1 is again
threatened), Bxc5; 4. Bxc5, g3; 5. b7, gxh2; 6. b8(Q, R or
B) and White mates next move.

(C) 1. . . . Bg7. 2. c5, Bc3; 3. Bh4 – the mixture as
before.

(D) 1. . . . Bf8. 2. c5, Bxc5 (this sacrifice is forced, as
the mate at e1 is again threatened); 3. Bxc5, g3 (if 3. . . .
a6, the continuation is 4. b6, as in (B) above); 4. Bd6 (the
mating threat is now Bc7), Kb6; 5. Bxf4 and White wins
easily by forcing home a queen's-side pawn.

Examples from Play: (3) Rook and Pawns

As stated previously, this type of ending is by far the most common, and the position in the diagram is as prosaic as one could wish for. In its banality lies its importance, however, for most players, as Black, would be content with a draw. This ending was reached in a match between players of international repute, and Black, far from being satisfied with a draw, perceived that by exact play a win could be forced. Every move is an object-lesson in timing and precision.

DIAGRAM 86

WHITE TO PLAY

White	Black
1. Rd7	

Preventing the advance of the black king.

1. . . .   **Rb3**

Cutting off the white king from the defence of the f-pawn.

2. Ra7   **Rd3**

Black's task is by no means easy. In general, a pawn plus in rook-and-pawn endings is of little importance if the pawns are all on one side of the board and the kings are in their own territories.

3. Rb7

White plays at "wait and see".

3. . . .   **Kg7!**

A profound move. If 3. . . . Kg6; 4. f5 ch., exf5 (4. . . . Kxf5; Rxf7 ch.); and Black although two pawns ahead, would have difficulty in winning for technical reasons too involved to discuss here.

4. Ra7   **h5**
5. Ra5   **Rd5**
6. Ra3

Of course, 6. Rxd5, exd5 would be instantly fatal for White. But after 6. Ra7, the subsequent play is not so easy: 6. . . . Kg6; 7. Re7 (not 7. f5 ch., as Black can now reply 7. . . . Rxf5; nor 7. Kf3, Rb5; 8. Ke4, Rb2; 9. f5 ch., Kf6!; arriving at a similar position to that in the game), Rb5; 8. Kf3, Rb3 ch., 9. Kf2, h4; 10. Kg2, Rb2 ch., 11. Kh3, Rf2; 12. Kg4, f5 ch.; 13. Kh3, Kf6 and with the white king temporarily out of the game, and with both the white rook and f-pawn *en prise*, Black is left with a simple win.

6. . . .	**Kg6**
7. Kf3	**Kf5**
8. h3	**h4**

An important move, as will be seen.

9. Rb3	**f6**

Now Black is able to stand a rook check without yielding ground and can concentrate on the weak h-pawn.

10. Ra3	**Rb5**

White's rook cannot leave the rank on account of the menace of a black rook check.

11. Rc3	**Rb2**

Threatening to win by Rh2 followed by Rxh3.

12. Rc5 ch.	**e5**
13. fxe5	**fxe5**

Now Black has obtained a passed pawn on the e-file.

14. Rc4	

Possibly Rc8 was slightly better here, but the scaffold is already erected.

14. . . .	**Rb3 ch.**

15.	Kg2	Rg3 ch.
16.	Kh2	

The only move to save the pawn. Now the black centre pawn is free to advance. If this pawn had been on the f-file, White could have saved the game (see note above). Black has calculated deeply.

16.	. . .	e4
17.	Rc8	e3
18.	Rh8	Rg6
19.	Rh5 ch.	

Not 19. Rxh4, e2; winning, nor 19. Re8, Re6; 20. Rf8 ch., Ke4; 21. Rf1, e2; 22. Re1, Ke3; 23. Kg1, Kd2; 24. Kf2, Rf6 ch.; followed by Kxel.

19.	. . .	Rg5
20.	Rh8	Kf4

20. . . . e2; would be a grave error, on account of Re8, winning the pawn and forcing the draw.

21.	Rxh4 ch.	Kf3
22.	Rh8	e2
23.	Re8	

Not 23. Rf8 ch., Ke4!; 24. Re8 ch., Re5.

23.	. . .	Rg2 ch.
24.	Kh1	Rf2
25.	Rf8 ch.	Kg3
26.	Resigns	

There is nothing to be done as the white rook must keep

checking because of Black's impending Rf1 ch. followed
by e1(Q). Now the black king comes back until the checks
are exhausted. For example, 26. Rg8 ch., Kh4; 27. Rh8
ch., Kg5; 28. Rg8 ch., Kh6; 29. Rh8 ch. (Rg1 is still met
by Rf1), Kg7; and White's rearguard action is over. An
instructive, if difficult ending.

Conclusion

A favourite query of the average chessplayer is – How
can I improve my play? It is a question the reader will be
asking sooner or later. The answer is simple – study the
end game. Practice will not make perfect, but it will go a
long way towards perfection – and in the ending the stakes
are high!

A few test positions are given. In problems of this
nature the phrase "to win" does not mean that analysis of

DIAGRAM 87   DIAGRAM 88

WHITE TO PLAY AND DRAW   WHITE TO PLAY AND WIN

DIAGRAM 89   **DIAGRAM 90**

WHITE TO PLAY AND WIN   WHITE TO PLAY AND WIN

DIAGRAM 91   **DIAGRAM 92**

WHITE TO PLAY AND WIN   WHITE TO PLAY AND WIN

play right up to the final mate is necessarily required, but only up to the point where victory is solely a matter of time. None of the examples is long, but each contains a "twist" that may occur in practical play.

Solutions

(87) 1. Ne6 ch., Bxe6; 2. Rf2, Qf7 (Qxf2 is stalemate); 3. Rxf7 ch., Kxf7 and Black cannot win (see "Bishop in Ending", Chapter 4).

(88) 1. g6, hxg6; 2. h6! Not 2. hxg6, Ke7; and Black wins. But 1. h6 (threatening g6), also wins for White.

(89) 1. Re1!, Rf2 (if 1. . . . Rxe1; 2. f8(Q) ch., Kc7; 3. Qc5 ch., Kd8; 4. Qa5 ch., winning the rook, or 3. . . . Kb7/8; 4. Qb4 ch., also winning the rook); 2. a3! (now Black is left without a waiting move and is said to be in "zugszwang". If Rg2 or Rh2, the pawn queens; whilst if the king moves, Ke7 wins), Rf1; 3. Rxe2, Rf3 (the rook cannot leave the file); 4. Rd2 ch., Kc8; 5. Rd5, Kc7; 6. Rf5, Re3 ch.; 7. Kf6 and queens next move.

(90) This is a very old ending. White, though a pawn down, is able to force a win. 1. a6!, Kb8 (to stop c7); 2. Kg1! (the only move; now the black king cannot move or one of the white pawns will queen, so a pawn is compelled to advance), f3; 3. Kf2 (White's strategy is to move the king in front of whichever pawn advances), h3; 4. Kg3 (now Black is in zugszwang; the pawns must be surrendered in turn after which the king must move to let by a white pawn), h2; 5. Kxh2, f2; 6. Kg2, g3; 7. Kf1, g2 ch.; 8. Kxf2, g1(Q) ch.; 9, Kxg1, Kc7; 10. a7, Kxc6; 11. a8(Q) wins.

(91) 1. Rc8 ch., Rxc8; 2. Qa7 ch!, Kxa7 (if 2. . . . Kc7; 3. bxc8(N) dis. ch., Kxc8; 4. Qxe7); 3. bxc8(N) ch., Kb7; 4. Nxe7, f4; 5. Nf5 and Black's pawns are decimated.

(92) 1. Ba1 (the only move), Kxa1; 2. Kc2, g5; 3. fxg5,

f4; 4. g6, f3; 5. g7, f2; 6. g8(Q), f1(Q); 7. Qg7 ch., Qf6;
8. Qxf6 mate.

8

ILLUSTRATIVE GAMES

The six master games that comprise this chapter have been chosen to illustrate the changing styles of play over the last century and a half. They range from the swashbuckling "Immortal Game", the positional mastery of Capablanca, the genius of Fischer, the technique of Karpov and the unrivalled creativity of the World Champion, Kasparov.

Game (1)
This game, played in London in 1851 between two of the leading players of the day, is popularly known as the Immortal Game. Typically, both sides attack, with White sacrificing in turn both rooks, a bishop, and finally the queen.

	White	*Black*
	Anderssen	Kieseritzky
1.	e4	e5
2.	f4	exf4

The King's Gambit. White has given up a pawn to gain

time and development.

3.	**Bc4**	**b5**

Striking at the weak square f7. Black returns the pawn to deflect the bishop.

4.	**Bxb5**	**Qh4 ch.**
5.	**Kf1**	**Nf6**
6.	**Nf3**	**Qh6**
7.	**d3**	**Nh5**
8.	**Nh4**	**c6**
9.	**Nf5**	**Qg5**
10.	**g4**	**Nf6**
11.	**Rg1**	**cxb5**

A sacrifice: the black queen now finds herself in a deal of trouble.

12.	**h4**	**Qg6**
13.	**h5**	**Qg5**
14.	**Qf3**	**Ng8**

Black's queen finds space at the cost of retarded development.

15.	**Bxf4**	**Qf6**
16.	**Nc3**	**Bc5**
17.	**Nd5**	**Qxb2**

This takes the queen away from the action. Sometimes called "the poisoned pawn", the b-pawn is frequently put on offer in modern opening play.

18.	**Bd6**	**Qxa1 ch.**

DIAGRAM 93

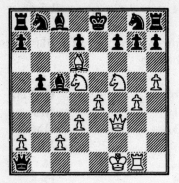

POSITION AFTER BLACK'S 18TH MOVE

The bishop moves into place for the mating net. Black now accepts the offer of the second rook.

19.	Ke2	Bxg1
20.	e5	Na6
21.	Nxg7 ch.	Kd8
22.	Qf6 ch.	

The final sacrifice.

22.	. . .	Nxf6
23.	Be7 mate	

Game (2)

The strategy in this game is clear-cut, White's superiority in space affording greater manoeuvrability for his pieces.

White	Black
Capablanca	Eliskases
1. e4	e5
2. Nf3	Nc6
3. Bc4	Bc5

The Giuoco Piano is considered a slow game, as its name implies: it is not popular in master play.

4. Nc3

Another good move here is c3.

4. . . .	Nf6
5. d3	d6

Decorous development: neither party interferes with the other – yet.

6. Bg5	h6

This move is important as White was threatening Nd5 followed by an exchange of pieces at f6, when Black would have been compelled to recapture with the pawn, creating serious structural weaknesses.

7. Bxf6	Qxf6
8. Nd5	Qd8

To guard against Nxc7 ch., winning the exchange, and also of course to rescue the queen.

9. c3

White sacrificed the two bishops (marginally stronger

than bishop and knight, remember) but in turn achieved quicker development. The text prepares to press home this advantage.

9. . . .	Ne7
10. Ne3!	

The move presents Black with a difficult problem since on 10. . . . 0–0; 11. d4, exd4; 12. Nxd4 White would command the centre.

10. . . .	Be6

This move is a mistake, as Capablanca demonstrates.

11. Bxe6	fxe6
12. Qb3	

Threatening two pawns.

12. . . .	Qc8
13. d4	exd4
14. Nxd4	Bxd4
15. cxd4	

The first phase may be said to be over. White, by unassuming moves, has gained a distinct advantage in the centre, a well-placed queen (against Black's passive one) and an open c-file for the white rooks.

15. . . .	0–0
16. 0–0	Qd7
17. Rac1	

If 17. Qxb7, Rfb8.

DIAGRAM 94

POSITION AFTER WHITE'S 15TH MOVE

| 17. . . . | Rab8 |

Necessary, since White was now threatening 18. Qxb7, and if 18. . . . Rfb8; 19. Qxc7.

| 18. Rc3 | d5 |
| 19. Qc2 | c6 |

19. . . . Nc6; would have given Black more counter-chances after 20. exd5, exd5; 21. Rc5, Nxd4; 22. Qd3.

20. e5	Rf4
21. Qd1	Rbf8
22. f3	Qd8
23. g3	R4f7
24. f4	Nf5
25. Nxf5	Rxf5
26. h4	

White has a pawn majority on the king's side whereas Black's queen's side majority has been rendered immobile. White controls more of the board and has a better pawn formation. Small considerations, perhaps, but enough for Capablanca to forge a win.

26. . . .	g6
27. Kg2	Qe7
28. a3	

White does not wish the black queen to exercise her nuisance value on the queen's wing.

28. . . .	Qg7
29. Rcf3	Qe7
30. Qc2	Kg7

Black awaits the gathering storm. After 31. g4, White threatened 32. Qxg6 ch.

31. g4	R5f7
32. Kh3	Qd7
33. b4	Rg8
34. Rg1	Kh8
35. Qd2	

Threatening f5.

35. . . .	Rh7
36. Qf2	h5
37. gxh5	Rxh5

If here 37. . . . gxh5; 38. Rg5, followed by a concentration of pieces on the g-file would be decisive.

38. Rg5	Qh7
39. Qg3	Qh6
40. Qg4	Rg7
41. Rg3	Kh7

On 41. . . . Rh7; 42. Rxh5, Qxh5; 43. Qxh5, gxh5; 44. Rg6, Re7; 45. Rh6 ch. would win.

42. Rg2

The object of this move is to bring the rook to the defence of the h-pawn and release the queen for action elsewhere.

42. . . .	Kg8
43. Kg3	Kh7
44. Rh2	Re7

For now White did threaten Qxe6.

| 45. Rh3 | Kg7 |

A weak move, but Black's hopes are fading. 45. . . . Re8 was better.

46. Rxh5	Qxh5
47. Qxh5	gxh5
48. f5!	

The break-through.

| 48. . . . | exf5 |
| 49. Kf4 | Re6 |

If 49. . . . Rf7; 50. Rg3 ch., Kh6; 51. Rg5.

50.	Kxf5	Rg6
51.	e6!	Rg4
52.	Ke5	Re4 ch.
53.	Kd6	Rxd4
54.	Re3	Resigns

The pawn must go through to queen.

Game (3)

This game demonstrates the folly of neglecting development and the safety of the king.

White	Black
Fischer	Geller
1. e4	e5
2. Nf3	Nc6
3. Bb5	a6
4. Ba4	d6
5. 0–0	Bg4
6. h3	Bh5

The ingenious sacrifice 6. . . . h5; is quite playable: if 7. hxg4, hxg4; the knight is attacked, and if it moves Black will threaten mate by 8. . . . Qh4.

7. c3	Qf6
8. g4	

This pawn advance in front of the castled king is usually dangerous; however Fischer has calculated that Black's king's side is uncoordinated.

8. . . .	Bg6
9. d4	Bxe4

White has sacrificed a pawn to open up the game.

10.	Nbd2	Bg6
11.	Bxc6 ch.	bxc6

The black king now has no shelter on the queen's side.

12.	dxe5	dxe5
13.	Nxe5	Bd6

Not 13. . . . Qxe5; because Black would lose his queen after 14. Re1.

14.	Nxg6	Qxg6
15.	Re1 ch.	Kf8
16.	Nc4	h5
17.	Nxd6	cxd6
18.	Bf4	d5?

This move loses quickly. Somewhat better might have been 18. . . . Rd8; 19. Qe2, hxg4; 20. hxg4 and Black is practically in zugszwang.

19.	Qb3	hxg4
20.	Qb7!	gxh3 dis. ch.
21.	Bg3	Rd8
22.	Qb4 ch.	Resigns

Black must lose knight and rook after 22. . . . Ne7; 23. Qxe7 ch., Kg8; 24. Qxd8 ch. See diagram 95 overleaf.

Game (4)

An example of a nicely-controlled king's-side attack. The players castle on opposite sides which usually makes for an exciting contest.

DIAGRAM 95

POSITION AFTER BLACK'S 19TH MOVE

White	*Black*
Karpov	Korchnoi
1. e4	c5
2. Nf3	d6
3. d4	cxd4
4. Nxd4	Nf6
5. Nc3	g6
6. Be3	Bg7
7. f3	

This is a sharp continuation in which White plans to castle queen's side and attack on the king's side.

7. . . .	Nc6

8.	Qd2	0–0
9.	Bc4	Bd7
10.	h4	Rc8
11.	Bb3	Ne5
12.	0–0–0	Nc4
13.	Bxc4	Rxc4
14.	h5	Nxh5

White has given up a pawn to clear the file for the king's rook.

15.	g4	Nf6
16.	Nde2	Qa5
17.	Bh6	

This is a favourite manoeuvre to get rid of a fianchet-toed bishop which here both defends the king and indirectly attacks White's castled position.

17.	. . .	Bxh6
18.	Qxh6	Rfc8
19.	Rd3	

It is necessary to defend the knight and consolidate the defence before launching the final attack on the king's side. Notice the black knight is tied to the defence of the h-pawn which is under pressure from the white queen and rook.

19.	. . .	R4c5
20.	g5	Rxg5

The black rook has been lured from its attacking position on the c-file.

21. Rd5	Rxd5
22. Nxd5	Re8
23. Nef4	Bc6

DIAGRAM 96

POSITION AFTER BLACK'S 23RD MOVE

| 24. e5! | Bxd5 |

If 24. . . . dxe5; 25. Nxf6 ch., exf6; 26. Nh5.

25. exf6	exf6
26. Qxh7 ch.	Kf8
27. Qh8 ch.	Resigns

. After 27. . . . Ke7; 28. Nxd5 ch., Qxd5; 29. Re1 ch. and White wins a rook or a queen for a rook.

Game (5)

In this game the centre is locked, both sides castle king's

side and seek play on opposite wings. This time it is Black who attacks on the king's side, and Kasparov finishes the game with a startling coup-de-grace.

	White Piket	Black Kasparov
1.	d4	Nf6
2.	Nf3	g6
3.	c4	Bg7

The "Indian" bishop is in place. White does not venture the Four Pawns Attack (see Opening 7) and instead develops circumspectly.

4.	Nc3	0–0
5.	e4	d6
6.	Be2	e5
7.	0–0	Nc6
8.	d5	

Locking the centre.

8.	. . .	Ne7
9.	Ne1	

In order to mobilise the f-pawn.

9.	. . .	Nd7
10.	Be3	f5
11.	f3	f4
12.	Bf2	g5
13.	b4	

White counter-attacks on the queen's side.

13. . . .	Nf6
14. c5	Ng6
15. cxd6	

Opening the c-file.

15. . . .	cxd6
16. Rc1	Rf7
17. a4	Bf8
18. a5	Bd7
19. Nb5	g4

If 20. fxg4, the white e-pawn is undefended.

20. Nc7	g3!

DIAGRAM 97

POSITION AFTER BLACK'S 20TH MOVE

21. Nxa8	Nh5

Maintaining the pressure. After 21. . . . gxf2 ch.; 22. Rxf2, Qxa8; White gains material but the attack disappears.

    22. Kh1

If 22. Bxa7, Qh4; and White cannot survive.

22. . . .	**gxf2**
23. Rxf2	**Ng3 ch.**

The knight can't be taken (24. hxg3, fxg3 with Qh4 ch. to follow).

24. Kg1	**Qxa8**
25. Bc4	

White still dare not take the knight.

25. . . .	**a6**
26. Qd3	**Qa7**
27. b5	**axb5**
28. Bxb5	**Nh1!**
Resigns	

Black wins rook for knight to secure a bishop-for-pawn advantage. See final position overleaf.

Game (6)

The best method of defence is often attack, particularly if a win is necessary. Britain is now in the top rank of chess-playing nations, and in this game the British Grandmaster Speelman shows why.

DIAGRAM 98

FINAL POSITION

White	Black
Timman	Speelman
1. e4	e5
2. Nf3	Nc6
3. Bb5	f5

An aggressive, but little-played line. 3. . . . a6, Nf6, or d6 are usual.

4. Nc3	fxe4
5. Nxe4	d5
6. Nxe5	dxe4
7. Nxc6	Qg5

Early fireworks, but this is a trodden path.

8. Qe2	Nf6
9. f4	

Defending the g-pawn. Notice that Black cannot capture *en passant* as Black's e-pawn is pinned.

9. . . .	Qxf4
10. Ne5 dis. ch.	c6
11. d4	Qh4 ch.
12. g3	Qh3
13. Bc4	

Better than 13. Nxc6.

13. . . .	Be6
14. Bg5	0–0–0
15. 0–0–0	

Both kings fly to safety.

15. . . .	Bd6
16. Nf7	Bxf7
17. Bxf7	Rhf8
18. Bc4	Rde8
19. d5	c5

After this move White's bishop has a bleak future.

20. Rhf1	Kb8
21. Bf4	Rd8
22. Bg5	a6

Preparing an eventual b5.

23.	Bxf6		gxf6
24.	Qxe4		Qxh2
25.	Rh1		Qxg3
26.	Rxh7		Rfe8
27.	Qf5		

This loses. White's only chance was 27. Qh4, Qf4 ch.;
28. Kb1.

27. . . .   b5

DIAGRAM 99

POSITION AFTER BLACK'S 27TH MOVE

28. Bf1

Otherwise the bishop is lost. If 28. Bb3, c4; and if
instead 28. Bd3, c4; 29. Be4, Qe3 ch.; etc.

| 28. . . . | Re1 |
| 29. Qh5 | |

If 29. Qd3, there follows 29. . . . Bf4 ch., 30. Kb1, Qxd3 winning.

29. . . .	Qf4 ch.
30. Kb1	Qxf1
Resigns	

9

GENERAL INFORMATION

This short chapter, in dealing with peripherals, ignores the title and the intention of the book.

A background of general information is desirable in any game however, and this is sufficient excuse for its inclusion.

Match Play

The first and paramount rule to remember in match play is that a chessman once touched must be moved; and that once a man is played (the move is completed on letting go of the man) the move stands.

It is a very good idea to keep to this rule in friendly games; there is little more annoying than the player who dithers when making a move. Decide on your move, execute it incisively, withdraw your hand.

If an opposing chessman is touched, the rule is that it must be captured if this is legitimately possible. If it is desired to centralize a man that has become misplaced, this can be done by saying *j'adoube* (Fr. "I adjust") before touching the man in question, and then only when it is your turn to move.

Matches and tournaments are decided on points – one point for a win, half a point for a draw.

In match play a time limit is normally imposed on the number of moves each player shall make in a prescribed period. Twenty to twenty-four moves an hour is usual, and if this time, which is allowed to each player (who is also permitted to think in the opponent's time) is exceeded, the player overstepping the time limit is ruled to have lost the game.

A chess clock is used to record the time taken by each player. This instrument consists of two ordinary clocks side by side connected by a lever which, when depressed, stops the clock on the one side and restarts it on the other; hence the two clocks never run simultaneously.

When you have made your move you press the lever thereby stopping your clock and setting your opponent's in motion. Should you omit to do this, your opponent will be thinking "free of charge".

Chess clocks have two small strips of metal, known as flags, fixed to the dials. They are so positioned that when the minute hand approaches the hour, it will push the flag up, releasing it exactly as the hour is passed, thereby eliminating any dispute that might otherwise have arisen as to whether or not the time limit had been exceeded.

Not all games may be concluded at the end of a match, when one of two courses is normally adopted:

(a) The game may be adjudicated (i.e., the result agreed upon) on the spot by the respective match captains, or by a strong player or players nominated by them. Often the game position is sent to an expert for a decision. Adjudications are common in team matches.

(b) The game may be adjourned, the players resuming when convenient. The procedure at adjournment is for the player whose move it is to write it down without making it on the board and without disclosing it. The clocks are then stopped and the game position, together with the clock times and the sealed move (often all on the one piece of paper) are put in an envelope. The envelope is sealed and the player who made the sealed move signs across the flap. The envelope is then given to the tournament director or to the second player to retain until the game is restarted. An illegal sealed move forfeits the game.

Players are permitted to analyse adjourned games. It is common practice but dubious ethics to seek advice at this stage.

Etiquette

It is not permitted in any way to disturb or distract a player during a game. In practice, this rule may prove difficult to interpret but it can be said that the player who is distracted is the best judge of what constitutes a distraction.

A player who resigns a game should obviously do so gracefully. Poor sportsmanship is unfortunately to be found in chess as it is in other games; one famous player wryly remarked that he had never won a game off a fit opponent!

Spectators should never pass audible comment on any match game in progress and nor should they interfere in any such game even if a breach of the rules has been committed.

Chess Clubs and British Chess

Chess clubs usually meet one or two evenings a week and apart from affording the opportunity for friendly games, offer various activities such as tournaments, matches against other clubs, etc. Most chess clubs are affiliated to their respective County Associations which in turn are affiliated to one or other of the regional Unions. These Unions, together with a few other independent bodies, send delegates to the British Chess Federation which is responsible for organised chess on a national basis.

A pleasing feature of chess life is that the traveller or holiday-maker is likely to find a welcome at the local club whether at home or abroad.

Congresses

A feature of chess in recent years has been the rise in popularity of the congress. A chess congress is an open tournament (usually a number of tournaments) covering anything from a day to a fortnight. Congresses are often arranged at resorts so that the competitor combines chess with a holiday. Normally one game is played each day, but in one-day and week-end events a fast time-limit, or a time-limit per game, is usual.

Chess Computers

In recent years the chess computer has become a popular opponent. Technical development in this field has been dramatic, and few players can now match the strength of the more advanced models. A chess computer is an always-ready opponent, capable of playing at a number of different speeds and levels, and usually offering a range of other facilities including advice on the best move, retracting moves, repeating games and solving problems. All computers have built-in opening repertoires. If no human guidance is at hand, a chess computer or software program, preferably the most advanced you can afford, is a recommended purchase.

Literature

Thousands of books have been written about chess,

covering the game in all its aspects. Most public libraries now offer a fair selection, but the average player will wish to have for his own use at least one book on the openings and one on the end game. These two books will be used mainly for reference and are essential for anyone who aspires to match or tournament play.

Two leading periodicals published in Great Britain are the *British Chess Magazine* and *Chess Monthly*. There are a number of other publications as well as scores of newspaper columns devoted to the game.

Famous Players

It is invidious to attempt this subject in a paragraph, but some players are so widely known, if only by name, even among non-players, that these at least deserve a mention.

Capablanca and Alekhine were two former world champions (and great rivals), but it was Steinitz, an earlier champion, who has probably contributed most to chess theory.

Except for the brief reign of an American, Bobby Fischer, the modern era has been dominated by the Russians with Karpov and Kasparov its present-day stars.

Britain, which now has a number of Grandmasters, has in recent years become a leading chess-playing nation.

Simultaneous Chess

Simultaneous displays are a feature of many clubs' activities. A master opposes a number of players (usually around twenty) at the same time.

Each player sits at a board. The master circulates and plays a move on every board. Players withhold their replies until the master returns to their table.

Time is heavily on the side of the challengers to begin with but this advantage is gradually reduced as the number of unfinished games diminishes.

Blindfold Chess

Many strong players are able to conduct one or more games without sight of the board. Moves are announced, and the blindfold player may or may not be literally blindfolded. The world record is over forty games played simultaneously in this fashion – an incredible achievement.

Correspondence Chess

Playing chess by post is popular among those who have time to spare or who are inhibited by domicile or infirmity from taking part in over-the-board activities. A correspondence game may last a few months or a few years and is a good way of improving one's powers of analysis.

There are many correspondence chess organisations, both national and international, and a player may of course participate in several matches and tournaments at the same time.

Chess Studies

Chess studies are often published in the Press. A study is a chess puzzle which the reader is invited to solve. There are three main types: the game position, the end game study and the problem. The game position is from actual play and the reader has to find the correct continuation. The end game study is contrived but is a plausible game position. The problem is another animal: it is artificial in appearance and in its most common form requires the reader to give checkmate with White in a specific number of moves. The chess problem is an art form, designed to puzzle and entertain, not to improve one's play.

Fairy Chess

Fairy chess covers in a general sense all those divertissements which are related to but deviate from the normal game. In this sense, the games mentioned in the following paragraph are Fairy chess. The term however is more commonly applied to problems. The artistic expression of the orthodox composer is severally constrained by the confines of the chessboard, the limitations of the regular chessmen and the rules of play.

In Fairy chess, the composer makes his own conditions. These may include the use of a different board, different men and different rules – sometimes all three in the same problem. Some wonderful work has been done in this field.

Other Games with the Chessmen

There are many digressive games possible with the normal chessmen.

Kriegspiel, Losing Game, Progressive Chess, Rifle Chess, Alice Chess – these are but a few. They are occasionally played in clubs and there is a specialist magazine, *Variant Chess*, published by the British Chess Variants Society.

Forsyth Notation

For taking down a position the Forsyth notation is unexcelled. Facing the board from White's side, squares and men are enumerated, starting at the top left-hand corner (a8) and working from left to right, rank by rank. White men are given in capitals, black in small letters.

The position in Diagram 9 (page 29) would thus be recorded: r3k2r/ (black rook, three squares, black king, two squares, black rook) pp5p/ (black pawn, black pawn, five squares, black pawn) 1P1Bn1p1/ (one square, white pawn, one square, white bishop, black knight, one square, black pawn, one square) 2pP4/1R6/1n3P2/P2p1KPP/ 1R3B2.

Descriptive Notation

The principal feature of the descriptive notation is that moves are recorded from the side of the player making them, so that each square has two descriptions, one for White, the other for Black.

The board is divided into files and ranks. Each file is named after the pieces (one on each side) that occupy it in the initial position. Thus the a-file is known as the queen's rook's (QR) file and the g-file as the king's knight's (KN) file. Ranks are numbered progressively 1–8 from the player. In the starting position each player's king stands on K1. Moves are recorded in the same way as in the short algebraic notation except that a dash is usually inserted between the initial of the man to be moved and the square to which it moves; also a pawn is always designated by its initial. For example, the opening moves 1. e4, e5; would be recorded in descriptive as 1. P-K4, P-K4.

Symbols are generally the same in the two systems, and ambiguities are resolved in a similar way. When capturing however it is the piece captured that is designated, not the square on which it stands. In diagram 100 the white move R4xb3 would be written by both White and Black as R(4)xN. The descriptive equivalent of white move axb3 would be RPxN or PxN(N3); PxN would not do, because it would not be clear which knight was captured. Where confusion cannot arise, the move can be abbreviated. The white move Bg3 is described simply as B-N3 – it is not necessary to say which bishop or which N3 square because only one is possible in each case.

The system is more cumbersome than the algebraic but has the merit of being linked to the starting position whereas the algebraic is abstract.

International Chess

The Fédération Internationale des Échecs (F.I.D.E.) is

the recognised world body responsible, *inter alia* for the World Championship and Chess Olympiad arrangements. F.I.D.E. has ruled that the algebraic notation must be used in all official events. Nearly all countries where chess is organised are members of F.I.D.E.

DIAGRAM 100

QR QN QB Q   K KB KN KR

8				♛			♜	1
7	♟	♟					♟	2
6		♙		♗	♞		♟	3
5			♟	♙				4
4		♖						5
3		♞				♙		6
2	♙			♟		♔	♙ ♙	7
1		♖				♗		8

QR QN QB Q   K KB KN KR

CHESS NOTATION

Master Titles

Grandmaster and International Master titles are conferred by F.I.D.E. from time to time on players whose performance in international events reached the required standard. Titles below this level (e.g., National Master, Candidate Master) are awarded by national chess authorities and vary from country to country. Only very strong players ever achieve recognition in this way.

Grading

Many countries now grade players who compete regularly in approved matches and tournaments and who attain a certain minimum standard.

A player's rating, or grading as it is commonly called, is derived from the aggregate of results over a period, the strength of the opponents being taken into account.

Gradings are used to determine qualification for national titles and, more widely, to assist in selection of players for matches and tournaments. They are also an incentive to the individual.

Other Notations

There are international codes for use in correspondence, radio, cable and telephone matches. Two letters or figures denote each square on the board, and a move is transmitted as a four-symbol group, the first two symbols indicating the square on which the man to be moved stands, the second two symbols the square to which it is to be moved. Checks and captures are not annotated.

INDEX

RIGHT WAY
PUBLISHING POLICY

HOW WE SELECT TITLES

RIGHT WAY consider carefully every deserving manuscript. Where an author is an authority on his subject but an inexperienced writer, we provide first-class editorial help. The standards we set make sure that every **RIGHT WAY** book is practical, easy to understand, concise, informative and delightful to read. Our specialist artists are skilled at creating simple illustrations which augment the text wherever necessary.

CONSISTENT QUALITY

At every reprint our books are updated where appropriate, giving our authors the opportunity to include new information.

FAST DELIVERY

We sell **RIGHT WAY** books to the best bookshops throughout the world. It may be that your bookseller has run out of stock of a particular title. If so, he can order more from us at any time – we have a fine reputation for "same day" despatch, and we supply any order, however small (even a single copy), to any bookseller who has an account with us. We prefer you to buy from your bookseller, as this reminds him of the strong underlying public demand for **RIGHT WAY** books. Readers who live in remote places, or who are housebound, or whose local bookseller is unco-operative, can order direct from us by post.

FREE

If you would like an up-to-date list of all **RIGHT WAY** titles currently available, please send a stamped self-addressed envelope to

ELLIOT RIGHT WAY BOOKS,
LOWER KINGSWOOD, TADWORTH,
SURREY, KT2O 6TD, U.K.

or visit our web site at www.right-way.co.uk